W9-BAF-912

COLLEGE SUCCESS GUIDE

TOP 12 SECRETS FOR STUDENT SUCCESS

SECOND EDITION

Dr. KARINE BLACKETT
PATRICIA WEISS

College Success Guide

© 2011 by Karine Blackett and Patricia Weiss

Published by JIST Works, an imprint of JIST Publishing
875 Montreal Way
St. Paul, MN 55102
Email: info@jist.com

Note to instructors. This book has support materials, including an instructor's guide CD. Visit www.jist.com for details.

About career materials published by JIST. Our materials encourage people to be self-directed and to take control of their destinies. We work hard to provide excellent content, solid advice, and techniques that get results. If you have questions about this book or other JIST products, visit www.jist.com.

Visit www.jist.com. Find out about our products, find job-search information, get free tables of contents and sample pages, order a catalog, and link to other career-related sites. You can also learn more about JIST authors and JIST training available to professionals.

Workbook Product Manager: Lori Cates Hand
Development Editor: Heather Stith
Cover Designer: Amy Adams
Interior Layout: Toi Davis
Proofreaders: Linda Seifert, Jeanne Clark
Indexer: Cheryl Lenser
Printed in the United States of America.
25 24 23 22 21 20 19   10 9 8 7 6 5 4

Library of Congress Cataloging-in-Publication Data

Blackett, Karine.
  College success guide : top 12 secrets for student success / Karine Blackett and Patricia Weiss. -- 2nd ed.
      p. cm.
  Includes bibliographical references and index.
  ISBN 978-1-59357-853-4 (alk. paper)
 1. Study skills--Handbooks, manuals, etc. 2. College student orientation--Handbooks, manuals, etc.
3. Success--Handbooks, manuals, etc. I. Weiss, Patricia. II. Title.
  LB2395.B317 2011
  378.1'70281--dc22
                                              2011010808

All rights reserved. No part of this book may be reproduced in any form or by any means, or stored in a database or retrieval system, without prior permission of the publisher except in the case of brief quotations embodied in articles or reviews. Making copies of any part of this book for any purpose other than your own personal use is a violation of United States copyright laws. For permission requests, please contact the Copyright Clearance Center at www.copyright.com or (978) 750-8400.

We have been careful to provide accurate information throughout this book, but it is possible that errors and omissions have been introduced. Please consider this in making any career plans or other important decisions. Trust your own judgment above all else and in all things.

ISBN 978-1-59357-853-4

College Success Is in Your Hands

Welcome! We are pleased that you picked up this book. You are holding the second edition of the *College Success Guide: Top 12 Secrets for Student Success*. We have taken the best practices of college students from around the country and world and compiled them for you along with useful tips, tools, and suggestions to make your college experience meet and exceed your wildest expectations. We are in the success business and want you to save time, money, and heartache by having these best practices at your fingertips.

Our book covers the experts' advice found to be truly helpful by all kinds of students—from the nontraditional students to those entering college directly from high school. Many of these students have families and full-time jobs, yet they found ways to have dynamic college experiences and succeed. That is our hope for you as well. Use these tools, not because the experts say they work, but because other learners have proved they work!

One outstanding feature of this book is that it offers more than one way to win. Chapter 11, for example, presents many excellent time management tools. If you are a procrastinator, you can use tools designed to motivate you; if you are a chronic planner, you can learn to bring more flexibility and synergy into your life so that you get more accomplished with ease.

We have incorporated digital media into this text, as well as interactive guided exercises, for you to find more success tools that are unique to you and your needs. That way, you can pull from many secrets of student success to get the most out of your education.

We have heard students say, "I have been trying so hard!" and what we say to you is, "Stop trying so hard." There's no need to continue spending your energy on inefficient efforts when there are tools available to help you succeed in college more easily and with better results. Just like crampons and carabiners make it easier to get to the top of a mountain, the academic tools presented in this book make it easier for you to get your diploma.

Dedication

I dedicate this book to my grandparents and parents: my father, Andrew Hubbeling; my stepmother, Carol Hubbeling; and my mother, Rev. Lin Jennewein, who instilled in me the love of learning and education. I also dedicate it to my son, Kevin, who now carries the learning torch.

—Dr. Kari Blackett

I dedicate this book to my late parents, Alice and Dale Johnson, who supported and encouraged me in all I have accomplished; my son, Louie, and my daughter, Alyce, who have made me proud to be a parent; my daughter in-law, Trish, and my son in-law, Fred, who have made our family complete; and last but not least to my grandsons, Gavin, Ethan, and Alex, who are my soul, my light, and my heart.

—Patricia Weiss

Acknowledgments

We would like to express our gratitude to President Dr. Jerry Gallentine and to the community of National American University for their commitment to the curriculum of The Pacific Institute and for their support of our careers and ideas. And thank you to other universities that have used this material with success, allowing the *College Success Guide* to assist their students in achieving their goals in college, career, and life.

We also thank Lou and Diane Tice, founders of The Pacific Institute, for their outstanding curriculum and their commitment to helping change lives and social systems for the betterment of all. Many thanks also to Dr. Joe Pace. These three were the change agents for many.

We also want to thank the people at JIST Publishing, who continue to see the value in this work.

Contents

Introduction

College Success Guide: Top 12 Secrets for Student Success can help you become more efficient and effective in studying. The 12 secrets it offers have enabled thousands of students to achieve far more than they originally believed possible.

How to Read This Guide

You do not need to read the chapters in this book in any order unless you are using it for a classroom text and your instructor has given you assignments. Otherwise, we suggest that you look over the table of contents to see which chapters you are most drawn to as well as which chapters you have the most resistance to reading. It may very well be that the ones that you would like to dismiss or skip are precisely the ones that you need the most at this point in your life. With this principle in mind, you may want to go to those chapters first to see what you are avoiding and what these chapters can bring into your life in a more positive way.

What Tools to Use

First, we suggest that you get a highlighter and mark the tips or best practices that you feel you can benefit the most from and do not want to forget. You may also want to highlight the website addresses that you want to visit, so they are easy to find. (You may want to use a second color for highlighting these items.)

Another suggestion is to complete the assignments in the chapters so you can see some benefits of the suggestions. There is a success principle behind this thinking. If you continue to plot out your life as you have been doing, you will continue to get the same results. You may be thinking that your way has served you just fine, and you do not want to rock the boat or get out of your comfort zone, so to speak. However, if you are willing to take a new approach, two wonderful things will happen, even if you later decide to go back to your old ways of managing your college experience.

First, you will shake up things in your subconscious enough that new ideas and creative energy will start to flow in other areas of your life. (This is also a reason you might want to drive a new way home now and then, or do something you usually don't do, like attending some social function.) The second reason for trying a new approach is that you may find that you had a blind spot in your old way and can now save more time or get more accomplished in less time. For these reasons, we suggest that you try a new approach for three weeks before you make a decision about whether it works for you.

What the 12 Secrets Offer

The *College Success Guide* was designed to give college and university students like you tried-and-true tools that you can implement on your own and get actual results from in a short amount of time. It is like having your own personal success coach guide you through the things highly successful students do. Following are the success secrets you will find in the chapters:

- **Chapter 1, Success Secret 1: "Study Skills."** Chapter 1 teaches you what high-performance learners do to study effectively. For example, you will learn how to increase your reading retention so you can spend less time reading and rereading the material. Other tools include chunking, symbols, and lists, as well as other study skills best practices.

- **Chapter 2, Success Secret 2: "Test-Taking Skills."** In Chapter 2, you learn how to manage test anxiety. Intelligence is largely what you can do effectively when you are under stress. Even if you have the knowledge, if you suffer from anxiety, your results can still be poor. You will also learn the test-taking secrets that students use to improve their performance on examinations.

- **Chapter 3, Success Secret 3: "Perception, Learning Styles, and Personality."** Discover an important, but often-overlooked truth: Not everyone learns the same way. Sometimes a teacher teaches using a method that is not conducive to the way you learn. If you struggle to understand the materials, the problem may not be that you are not smart enough to master the topic. It may be that you learn better when you approach the material from a different angle.

So are you doomed? Not at all. Chapter 3 will help you identify how you learn best, so you can get the most out of your classes regardless of how the material is presented or whether your class is on campus or online.

- **Chapter 4, Success Secret 4: "Organization."** Is there a way to become organized so you get better results in college? You bet there is. Chapter 4 gives you the organization techniques students have used for better performance.

- **Chapter 5, Success Secret 5: "Attitude."** William James said, "A human being can alter his life by altering his attitude." Chapter 5 teaches you how to use the power of your thoughts and attitude to get the results you seek in your college experience. You can use these simple tools and get better results immediately.

- **Chapter 6, Success Secret 6: "Goal Setting."** Unique to humans is the fact that without goals there is, in essence, no life. Up to this point, you have been using goal setting either by purposeful design or by default. You will know if you have been setting goals by default because you do not have the things that you hoped for, wanted, and desperately desired. Rather, you find yourself wondering why others seem to have more or do more than you have or do. You also may feel that you try hard, often really hard, with little result or with challenges. If these statements sound familiar, then Chapter 6 is for you.

- **Chapter 7, Success Secret 7: "Basic Research Skills."** Just as most of us need a recipe to make a terrific gourmet dish, most students need a recipe to do excellent research. Without such a recipe, students may spend a great deal of time and energy gathering data and end up with very little material or a great deal of poor-quality material. This chapter takes you beyond an Internet search and gives you simple ways to do awesome research. Chapter 7 is your personal recipe for doing great research.

- **Chapter 8, Success Secret 8: "Research Paper Writing."** Much like the recipe for successful research, there are best practices for writing outstanding research papers. Chapter 8 gives you the best tips and tools for writing excellent research papers. It also shares the addresses of websites that walk you through the writing process. In essence, you will have a coach by your side to help you make the process of writing a research paper less like a chore and more like baking a cake (and a boxed one, to boot).

- **Chapter 9, Success Secret 9: "Synergy."** You don't have to go it alone with your college experience. You can use the energy and resources of all sorts of helpful individuals—your classmates, instructors, librarians, and tutors. You also have access to other support people who are ready and willing to assist you, if you learn to ask. Chapter 9 shows you how to network in college to make your "effort of one" multiply so that you reap the synergistic "results of many."

- **Chapter 10, Success Secret 10: "Motivation."** If you find that you are trying hard with little to show for your efforts, check out Chapter 10. It takes away the guesswork and reveals what you are doing wrong. Using the motivation rules, tools, and principles in this chapter will make getting the job done or even just getting start ed look easy.

- **Chapter 11, Success Secret 11: "Time and Energy Management."** We all get the same 24 hours in a day. No more and no less. However, some students use their time so effectively that it seems they have more to spare for things they enjoy. Is it magic? No! They know the secrets of planning their time for better results. The amazing thing is that it is not beyond anyone's reach to mimic what these students are doing to get the same excellent results. Best of all, for all you procrastinators, Chapter 11 shares ways you can turn your procrastination into a success tool!

- **Chapter 12, Success Secret 12: "Stress Management."** Without some stress, your life would not have much meaning. The goal is to have the optimum level of stress in which you are effective and productive, yet healthy and balanced. Chapter 12 will give you the tools to learn how to increase the threshold of the amount of stress you can gracefully and productively endure.

The appendix is your guide to finding even more details about the success secrets and best practices outlined in this book.

We wish you great success on your journey and want you to know that you are not alone. We—and thousands of other successful students—are cheering you on.

CHAPTER 1

Study Skills

"The purpose of studying is learning the material, not just memorizing it."

Anonymous

No matter how much you want to go deep sea diving, you cannot do it successfully if you do not have the right training and tools. The same is true for academic success. You need the right tools for the job. In this chapter, we take a look at some effective study skills.

Reading Tools

The following sections present tools that can assist you in becoming a more efficient and productive reader. If you use these tools while reading, you will become a much better student, and you will find studying for tests to be less difficult than it was in the past.

Get the Correct Textbook

Pay close attention to the edition of the textbook listed on the syllabus for your class. You may be tempted to purchase a less expensive used textbook and may accidentally get an earlier edition rather than the required one.

Publishers come out with new editions because content has changed or new material has been added. In the new edition, authors may update cases and content to reflect trends and changes in the subjects covered. Students who purchase earlier editions are then surprised to find that the class lecture doesn't match what they have read. They are especially surprised when they turn in an assignment based on a case study in Chapter 2 or answered the questions at the end of the chapter and discover that all their answers are wrong because the case studies and questions are entirely different in the new edition of the book.

This doesn't mean you can't purchase a used book if it is the correct edition. Just make sure the edition of the textbook you purchase is the one being used.

Previewing

When you preview material, you focus on titles, headlines, topic sentences, the first sentences in the paragraphs, the introduction, and the conclusion. By reading these items, you should gain a basic understanding of the topic and main ideas.

Prereading

Prereading uses skimming and scanning techniques to grasp an awareness of the entire passage in a "nutshell." You do not read each word, but you search for the overall structure and content of the material before you read for comprehension. By prereading, you focus on what is essential and save a great deal of time.

When you are prereading, you are seeking the main topic and the general ideas of the material. You are not reading for content specifics. What you need to search for and read are these items:

- Book title
- Chapter titles
- Headings or objectives
- Anything that is italic, bold, highlighted, or in larger print

- Maps, charts, and diagrams
- First and last sentence of each paragraph
- Anything in a box, underlined, or somehow set off for your eyes to catch
- First and last paragraph and summary of a passage

The difference between skimming and scanning in prereading is important. When you skim, you do not read every word. You let your eyes move quickly over the sentences and get a feel for what is being said. When you scan, you think ahead about what you are searching for and search for it.

Skimming

Skimming allows you to become familiar with the organization and general content of the material you are going to read. To skim effectively, follow these steps:

1. Read the title and section headings.
2. Read the titles of any maps, charts, or graphs.
3. Read the entire introduction.
4. Read the first sentence of each section or paragraph.
5. Read the last paragraph or summary.

Keep in mind that you are skimming for the main idea. As you read, ask yourself these questions: Who? What? When? Where? Why? How? Doing so puts you in a critical frame of mind and enables you to identify the main points.

Scanning

When you scan, you are searching for specific information within a text without reading the entire text. This process involves looking for keywords, special typographical features (such as bullets, bold, italic, and so on), or any other features that highlight facts. If you want to know where the story takes place, for example, you search for a location or place. You let your eyes move quickly until you come across this information. When you scan material, look for the main idea of the book, chapter, section, and paragraph.

If you need more information on how to preview and preread by skimming and scanning, enter those words in a search engine on the Internet; you will find more ideas and practice tips.

Combining Previewing and Prereading

Try out some proven approaches that combine previewing and prereading for improving your reading skills and retention. One method that students have found particularly helpful is called PQR3. In this method, you

- Preview what you will learn from the material.

- Question what you will learn.

- Read the selection.

- Recite what you are learning in your own words periodically as you read.

- Review what you have read when you are finished.

Another method is SQRW. This method is particularly helpful for reading textbooks:

- Survey by thinking about what you already know on the topic.

- Question what you will learn.

- Read the selection.

- Write the questions and answers in your notebook.

Using this method, you become familiar with the content, chapter headings, key charts, and diagrams. You repeat this process with each subsequent chapter.

For more details on this method, you can type "SQRW" into your favorite search engine or go to this page at How-to-Study.com:

www.how-to-study.com/pqr.htm

Highlighting and Annotating

You may have been conditioned to the rule "Do not write in books" from the time you were small until you were out of high school. Now that you're in college, you're encouraged to highlight and write in those textbooks. It's okay. You own your textbooks now. (If you are borrowing or renting your books, however, put the highlighter away and make your notes in a separate notebook.) Don't be traumatized. It can be quite a "highlighting" experience.

> **Note:** If you use e-books, make sure you explore the highlighting and note-taking functions available in the programs or e-readers you use to display the books. Spending time now to learn how to use these features effectively will pay off when you have to use these books to study for tests.

Completely read a chapter before you start marking and highlighting. When you do highlight, follow these guidelines:

- **Be selective.** Don't underline or jot down everything. When you put notes in the margins, use your own words.

- **Be brief.** Underline meaningful phrases rather than complete sentences.

- **Be quick.** You don't have all day for marking. Read, go back for a mini-overview, and make your markings. Then attack the next portion of the chapter.

- **Be neat.** Neatness takes conscious effort, but doesn't require additional time. In fact, neatness can save time later because you won't waste time figuring out what you scribbled or wrote.

As you read and make notes, organize facts and ideas into categories. Try cross-referencing information, identifying pointers to other places in the same document or to other information sources where you can find related information.

Note-Taking Tools

Taking notes doesn't have to be difficult. Make it easy on yourself. Have two systems: one for taking notes in class and the other for creating notes for reviewing facts you need to learn.

Taking Lecture Notes

If you remember these simple note-taking tips, note-taking in your courses can become less challenging. You will find that your success rate will continue to rise.

- **Use a laptop.** Many students have laptops that they take with them to class. If you are a quick typist, using your laptop to take notes is a great idea. Such notes tend to be much cleaner and easier to read. If your professor provides class materials electronically, you can keep everything in a folder instead of having to keep track of a lot of papers. Remember to back up your work on a regular basis so you don't lose anything!

- **Keep all your handouts and notes for a class in a three-ring binder.** If you have no laptop, or if your professor still uses paper, use a three-ring binder for keeping lecture notes, handouts, and your notes from the textbook and other reading. You are less likely to spend time hunting for important documents if they are all in one place. You can arrange pages with lecture notes and corresponding handouts next to each other. If you miss a lecture, you can easily add the missing notes in the right place after copying them from a classmate. Make sure to date and number your handouts to keep them in order.

- **Leave space while taking notes to help you when you review them later.** Write your notes in pen and use only one side of your paper. Doing so will make them easier to read. Give yourself extra blank space in your notes and plenty of room to write. Use paper that has a wide margin on the left side. If you can't find paper with a wide margin, draw it. Write your notes on the right side of the margin line. You can then use the left margin when reviewing your notes.

- **Take as many notes as you can during class.** If you miss something, leave a space. You can fill it in later. Do not stop taking notes if you become lost or confused. Add a question mark and leave a space; you can come back to what you missed later.

- **Free yourself of worries about punctuation.** Taking time to decide what punctuation you need and then writing or typing it is unnecessary.

- **Use signs, texting codes, and abbreviations as much as possible (see the "Tips for Taking Notes" box).** Some students have a fear of forgetting what abbreviations and symbols mean. But after you get into the habit of using them, you won't forget.

Tips for Taking Notes

Use common symbols and graphics:

=	equal	≠	does not equal
*	important	**	very important
>	greater than	<	less than
w/	with	w/o	without
&	and	#	number
$	cost, money	(),{},[]	information that belongs together

Use common abbreviations:

cf	compare	eg	for example	dept	department
vs	versus	mx	maximum	ɪɪɪɪ	minimum
NYC	New York City				

Use the first syllable of a word:

bus   business   pol   policy

Eliminate final letters; use just enough to recognize the abbreviation:

info   information   assoc   association

Use apostrophes to abbreviate words:

gov't   government   cont'd   continued

Omit vowels from the middle of words:

bkgrd   background   estmt   estimate

- **Work with your notes as soon as you can after class.** You can organize them and make them clearer while they are still fresh in your mind.

- **As you review your notes, look at the information as answers to questions.** As these questions become clear to you, type them into your document on the laptop or jot them, as well as keywords, in the left margin of your paper. Then you can recall the information by covering up the right side of your notes and testing yourself.

Reviewing with Note Cards

Note cards are great for learning terminology and presenting written information out of sequence. Creating and using note cards can alleviate anxiety about remembering facts and can be a valuable portable study tool. Follow these steps:

1. Start compiling cards at the beginning of the quarter or semester.

2. As you review your class notes or reading material, write each term or question you need to memorize on a 3x5 card.

3. On the other side of each card, write the definition, description, or answer.

4. Carry the cards with you and review them often—while standing in line, waiting for an appointment, waiting for a ride, and so on. Repetition is the best way to learn some material, and note cards let you readily review the information time and again.

Study Tools

An assignment in Chapter 3, "Perception, Learning Styles, and Personality," is to take a learning assessment to determine your learning style. The goal of an assessment is to know yourself well enough to recognize your study strengths and weaknesses. You are likely to have the most success using study tools that match your learning style and study strengths. The sections that follow explain several different study techniques. Try them all to find the ones that work best for you.

For more information on study tools, visit the Study Guides and Strategies website. This site has a variety of study tools designed to make you a more effective and efficient learner:

www.studygs.net

Chunking

There's only so much information you can hold in your short-term memory (about seven things, according to a study published in the 1950s by psychologist George Miller). To move information from your short-term to your long-term memory so that you can recall it later, it's helpful to organize a big mass of information into small chunks of related information.

This book, for example, uses subheadings, bulleted lists, and other chunking methods to present information in a way that is easier to understand and find again later. A book presented in one long block of text would be difficult to read!

If you are a visual learner (see Chapter 3), chunking could be an especially effective tool for you. By creating a mental picture or drawing a diagram that represents several ideas or facts, you create one chunk of information that you have to remember, which is much easier than trying to remember several separate pieces. This type of chunking is effective because people remember pictures more easily than words.

You can find out more about chunking by googling the keyword "chunking" and at the following website:

www.ababasoft.com/mnemonic/tech02.htm

MURDER

Students seem to have an affinity for the MURDER approach to improving study skills. MURDER stands for:

- **<u>M</u>ood.** Be in the correct mood for studying.

- **<u>U</u>nderstand.** Understand what you are learning or highlight it so you can learn it better later.

- **<u>R</u>ecall.** Recall the information in the section you are studying before you move on.

- **Digest.** Integrate what you have learned.
- **Expand.** Expand the knowledge you have gained.
- **Review.** Review what you have studied.

The Study Guides and Strategies site is well worth visiting to learn more about the MURDER technique of studying:

www.studygs.net/murder.htm

Mnemonic Devices

Mnemonic devices are aids for improving one's memory. These devices can be great for memorizing information. They generally attach new information to be learned to old information already mastered or to catchwords or phrases that are easily remembered. If you need to memorize the colors of the spectrum, for example, you can remember the name Roy G. Biv. Red, orange, yellow, green, blue, indigo, and violet are the colors of the spectrum.

The following sections present three mnemonic devices: jingles, acronyms, and acrostics. If you review these helpful tools often, they can help you become a success in class.

Jingles

Jingles are rhyming phrases sometimes put to song. Many people have used a common jingle to memorize the number of days in each month. You can use this jingle for accounting and business math concepts when you need to remember how many days are in a month in calculating discounts on notes and interest:

Thirty days has September,

April, June, and November.

All the rest have 31,

Except February alone,

Which has 28 days clear

And 29 in each leap year.

Memorize that jingle, and you will remember the number of days in each month forever. Make up jingles for other things you need to memorize.

Acronyms

Acronyms are catchwords. For example, HOMES is the catchword for learning the Great Lakes—Huron, Ontario, Michigan, Erie, and Superior. And CANU is the catchword for naming the only spot in the United States where four states meet: Colorado, Arizona, New Mexico, and Utah.

To create an acronym, write the information you need to remember in a list, number the list, and then underline the first letter in each word to see whether you have a recognizable catchword. Say you need to remember the four symptoms of schizophrenia for a psychology course. Begin by making a list of the symptoms:

1. withdrawal

2. hallucinations

3. inappropriate emotional response

4. delusions

When you underline the first letter of each symptom, you get the catchword *whid*. Whid is easy to say and easy to remember and will trigger the names of the four symptoms when you think of it.

Using a silly acronym can help you to remember your catchword and the information attached to it. The important thing is that it helps you to become a better student.

Acrostics

Acrostics are catchphrases. The steps for developing acronyms and acrostics are the same.

Say you need to memorize these seven diatomic molecules for chemistry class:

1. <u>b</u>romine

2. <u>h</u>ydrogen

3. <u>c</u>hlorine

4. <u>f</u>luorine

5. <u>o</u>xygen

6. <u>n</u>itrogen

7. <u>i</u>odine

To create a catchphrase for this list, begin by underlining the first letter of each molecule. Then make up a phrase, such as "<u>B</u>rian <u>h</u>elps <u>C</u>laire <u>f</u>ind <u>o</u>ut <u>n</u>ew <u>i</u>deas."

Mind Maps

At the end of each section of reading or your notes, recall the main ideas involved and start creating or adding to your own mind map. A *mind map* is a diagram of the connections you make between ideas.

To make a mind map, you can use drawing software or colored pencils and a blank sheet of paper. Follow these steps:

1. Write the topic you are studying in the center of the page.

2. Draw a branch from that center topic for each main idea that relates to it. Some people find it helpful to make each branch a different color.

3. Add branches for subtopics for each of the main ideas. Use short phrases or symbols to represent each idea.

4. Review your mind map in intervals: Immediately after you study, again in 24 hours, after one week, and then in one month. Add to it or change it as necessary.

For more information on mind maps, go to James Cook University's Study Skills Online site:

www.jcu.edu.au/tldinfo/learningskills/mindmap

Online Class Tools

The study skills you need if you are an online student are the same as those stated throughout this chapter. You may not have to do a lot of note-taking, but the skills will come in handy anyway. Trust us.

> **Note:** Your keyboarding skills will improve as you go online for your classes. If you are a slow keyboarder, you can practice keyboarding or take a class, but you will become faster as you go. You can also check out a typing book from your local or school library and practice your typing skills.

In addition, hundreds of successful online students have identified certain tools you can use to improve your ability to handle anything that comes your way in the online environment. These are explained in the following sections.

Handling the Technology

Of greatest importance are the computer and Internet connection. This may seem basic, but without them, you have no class! Check your school to find the minimum hardware and software requirements. Many online schools have a simple link you can click from your computer that will scan your computer for you and diagnose what you are missing. The link is often called a *system check*.

If you can afford it, go beyond the minimum requirements. Successful online students have nearly unanimously commented that you should not skimp on technology. The extra money you spend up front on faster hardware and Internet technology will be recouped in short order with substantial savings of time.

Know what equipment will be needed and make sure that you have access to this equipment on a regular basis. Here are some issues to consider:

- If you are behind a firewall, such as on a military base, make sure your IT people grant you access to the URL address for your class.

- Make sure that your Internet connection is working before the class starts, and know what Internet browser and browser settings you need to take your course. Some online learning management systems perform better in one browser over another. In other words, you might want to try more than one browser to reach your class. For example, you might have both Internet Explorer and Mozilla Firefox ready on your PC as Internet connections.

- If you have a program that disables "pop-ups" on your computer, you may want to enable pop-ups. Some course platforms need the pop-up function for you to send mail in class. Ask your school about this issue.

Although you don't need to be a computer wizard, you will want to have or be willing to learn basic computer skills so that the process is less frustrating. Do not let the lack of computer skills deter you, however; many successful online students could only send e-mail when they enrolled. Your willingness to learn will be the key to your success. Hitting a learning curve can be frustrating or even daunting at times, but your willingness to try quieting your mind and allowing the new thoughts to come in can take you far. Asking for help and calling the tech support hotline will get you ahead of the game as well.

Getting the Required Materials

You will still need to get a textbook and other required material. Do not overlook this point and think you can get away without required materials. Get the textbook and get it early. We cannot tell you how many students we have watched drop their online classes, which cost them dearly, because they waited too long to buy, rent, or borrow the correct textbook. Somehow they thought that it would be okay if they did not have the textbook, that somehow their teacher would give them an extension or send them the chapters. Wrong.

Note: Sometimes reading assignments will be displayed in the condensed format—that is, they will be summarized—and the entire reading assignment will not be shown online. As an online student, your reading materials may also be in the classroom as an e-book or online instructional material. When you register for the course, ask whether you need to order the textbook or whether it is online in the classroom.

In fact, many online learning management systems do not even allow instructors to accept late assignments or quizzes. When the week is closed, you can view it, but the classroom technology shuts off the students' ability to post assignments or add to discussions. So get your books early.

This also applies to any software you may need to get for your course. Get what is required and get it soon. The more time you have to familiarize yourself with the intricacies of software, such as word processing programs and spreadsheets, the better. Some software will be freeware. For example, you can download Adobe Reader for free to read PowerPoint presentations:

http://get.adobe.com/reader/

You might also find that you can download a free converter file to read other versions of Word documents.

Another website to check out is OpenOffice.org. *Open Office* is the leading open-source software suite for word processing, spreadsheets, presentations, graphics, and databases, and it is free:

www.openoffice.org

The last thing you want is to fail before you have a chance to succeed. So get your basic tools ready and use your books and supplement material as intended.

Being Proactive

Preview the material before you go online. Do all optional assignments to make your online time more effective. This is part of being fiercely responsible for yourself.

Once you are online, take the time to click on illustrations, examples, definitions, and other links. This way you enrich your understanding and solidify what you are learning.

Be curious about your online class and explore it. Try new computer commands in the course to fully learn how to navigate. You can learn a great deal about your course structure by punching buttons and seeing where they lead you.

Conclusion

Having the materials and technology you need, knowing how to read and take notes effectively, and learning strategies for studying are all recognized as extremely important by successful students and teachers alike. There really is no excuse for any student to do anything but succeed in an on-campus or online environment with this information. Becoming a successful student just takes a little elbow grease, and we guarantee it will pay off.

Best Practices: Study Skills

Do

- Do get your textbooks in advance.

- Do make sure you know how to access materials that are online. Whether you are on-campus or online, it's to your benefit to get a head start.

- Do use skimming, scanning, and other reading strategies. Doing so pays off in time savings and better grades every time.

- Do take time to work on your learning skills. Making the transition from teacher-centered learning (in which the focus is on the teacher) to learner-centered learning (focusing on the learner) is important. In other words, how you learn, your particular learning style, is essential to your success. Make sure to discover your learning style and use it to your advantage.

- Do get the best computer hardware and software, especially if you are an online student. If you don't, you probably have a long and tough road ahead of you. It is better to spend a few extra dollars than be sorry. Having a laptop is recommended.

- Do have a reliable and high-speed (if available) or broadband Internet service, a time-saving feature that pays for itself day after day.

Don't

- Don't start class without having all the books, technology, and other materials you need to be successful.

- Don't underestimate your ability to learn. Tools will help you finish the job successfully.

- Don't use absolutes of "can't," "won't," or "never." You can and will if you simply try. Repeat this statement often: "I can do this."

Assignment 1.1: Find Study Skills Information on the Web

In this assignment, you search the Web for additional information about improving your studying skills.

1. Visit three websites on study skills, either by choosing them from the list below or the URLs for this chapter at the end of the book or by conducting your own Internet search with the keywords "study skills":

   www.how-to-study.com

   www.jcu.edu.au/tldinfo/learningskills/mindmap

   www.studygs.net

   www.studyguidezone.com

   www.ababasoft.com/mnemonic/tech02.htm

2. Find six study techniques or tips that interest you. Make a list of the URLs you selected and the six tips you found.

   URL: _____

   Tip: _____

   URL: _____

   Tip: _____

   URL: _____

   Tip: _____

   URL: _____

   Tip: _____

   URL: _____

   Tip: _____

   URL: _____

   Tip: _____

(continued)

(continued)

3. Briefly describe your thoughts on each of these tips. Explain why they appeal to you. Include the reasons you find the tips helpful and whether you plan to use them.

_____

_____

_____

_____

_____

_____

_____

_____

_____

_____

_____

_____

_____

_____

_____

_____

_____

_____

Assignment 1.2: Practice Study Skills

In this assignment, you practice some of the study skills you have learned. Choose one of your classes in which you are challenged. Apply the study skills to that class from now until you take your first exam in that class. You should do the following:

1. Read the chapters or units before they are discussed in class.

2. Practice the skimming and scanning reading tips.

3. Review the note-taking tips that you read in this chapter.

4. Jot down notes while you read.

5. Jot down questions you have about the information you read.

6. When you get to class, focus on some of the objectives that were listed in the beginning of the chapter. Listen for key terms. Now is the time to use your note-taking skills. Practice taking notes each class period before the exam.

7. When the instructor asks for questions during or at the end of the lecture, ask those questions you jotted down earlier.

8. Find out when the first exam will be and what type of exam will be given.

9. Read over the chapter for the second time, focusing on the terms and ideas that the instructor stressed during class.

CHAPTER 2

Test-Taking Skills

*"There's no such thing as a stupid question,
but they're the easiest to answer."*

Tech Support Guy at www.techguy.org

Taking tests can be scary. However, tests are something you can't get away from. For you to earn your degree, the school has to have some way of knowing you understand the material in your classes. Your instructors have to test you to see whether you learned anything.

Test Preparation Tools

The key to the process of successful test-taking lies in time management. Successful students start preparing for exams on the first day of class. You can do this by reading the syllabus. You need to know how many exams you have, their point values, and when they will take place.

Some exams are timed; if the allotted time is not obvious, you will want to ask your instructor how much time is allotted for each exam. Often online courses will turn on and off at specific times. (If an exam is an online test, find out whether you have unlimited time or it is timed.) Find out what time zone the syllabus refers to and the test dates.

Also, ask what type of exams you will be taking. Are they open book? Are the questions mostly multiple choice or all essay? Knowing the type of test will help you to study more efficiently.

Transfer all of this information into your cell phone, laptop, iPad, and/or calendar. Then you will be thinking of your exams and reviewing for them throughout the entire course rather than just one exam at a time.

Review for several short bursts rather than one long period. Your review is much more than just rereading the lecture notes and the assignments. Watch for hints from your instructor. If the instructor says, "You should know the following information," or if the instructor repeats something more than once, you can be assured that you probably will see it again in an exam. If the instructor reviews for an exam on a certain day, make sure you are there. If you miss class during the review, get the review notes from a classmate.

Get together with students in your class and form a study group. You can even connect with other online students by e-mailing them or using the student lounge if there is one. These reviews can reinforce your learning. If you cannot be part of a study group, at least have a buddy available to call or e-mail if you are stuck. Don't forget that you can contact your instructor as well. The more people you have to support you and help you, the better.

Try to predict what will be asked on the exam, and then outline your responses. Don't be afraid to ask your instructor whether certain material will be on the exam.

Depending on the course material, you may want to use old-fashioned flashcards. It has been reported that you must hear or see something about eight times to learn and remember it. That is the beauty of flashcards. You will be relearning the material simply by making the flashcards and then reviewing them.

Test-Taking Tools for Specific Types of Questions

This section lists some great test-taking tools for specific types of exam questions. You will be surprised how much better you will do on tests if you review these tools several times during the quarter or semester.

Remember, the more you see or hear something, the more you will remember it. If you use these tools, you can increase your grade by 10 points or more.

True/False Question Tools

The following are tools you can use when your exam has true/false questions.

- **Determine the number of questions and budget your time.** Usually, an exam that contains true/false questions has many of them. If so, answer each question quickly. It may not be worth a lot of time to get one question right if it is worth only 2 points on a 100-point test.

- **Read each question carefully.** Remember that if any part of a statement is false, the entire statement is false. Most questions contain a combination of who, what, when, where, or how facts. If any one of these facts is wrong, the statement is false.

- **Look for qualifiers.** Words such as never, all, none, and always generally indicate a statement is false. Words and phrases such as on the other hand, sometimes, generally, often, frequently, and mostly indicate a statement is true.

- **Answer the questions you know first.** Often answers to questions you don't know are supplied in other questions. Go back and answer difficult questions last.

- **When guessing, do not change answers.** Research indicates that your first answer is usually right. However, don't be afraid to change answers when you have good reason to do so.

- **Know that "reason" statements tend to be false.** When something is given as the "reason" or "cause" or "because of" something else, the statement tends to be false.

- **Answer all questions.** Unless points are deducted for incorrect responses, leave enough time to answer all questions. Mark all remaining or unanswered questions as true. In a true/false exam, a slight majority of the answers are usually true.

Multiple-Choice Question Tools

You can use the following tools when your exam has multiple-choice questions:

- **Attempt to answer the question without looking at the options.** If necessary, cover the answers with your hand.

- **Eliminate the distracters, those answers that you know are obviously wrong.** Cross those out.

- **Analyze the options as true/false questions.** In a negatively worded question (for example, which of the following are not), put a T or F beside each option, and then select the false statement.

- **Never be afraid to use common sense in determining answers.** It is sometimes easy to confuse yourself by attempting to recall the right answer rather than simply reasoning through the question. Make sure your answer makes sense.

- **Answer the questions you know first.** Often answers to questions you don't know are supplied in other questions. Go back to answer the difficult questions later.

- **When guessing, do not change answers.** Research indicates your first answer is usually best. However, don't be afraid to change answers when you have a good reason for doing so.

- **When guessing, choose answers that are not the first or last option.** Research indicates that the option in the middle with the most words is usually the correct response.

- **If the first option is a correct one, look at the last option to make sure it is not an "all of the above" option.** Likewise, if the first option is wrong, check for a "none of the above" option.

- **Answer all the questions.** Unless points are deducted for incorrect responses, guess if you have to in order to answer all the questions.

- **Allow time at the end to check your answers and correct careless mistakes.**

Short-Answer or Fill-in-the-Blank Question Tools

There are few, if any, "tricks" for short-answer or fill-in-the-blank exam questions. If, however, you know an exam will have these types of questions, there are some strategies you can use to prepare:

- Overstudy—that is, study more than you think you need to. Often the difference between an A and a B grade boils down to just a little more effort or review.

- Focus on facts and keywords.

- Look over your materials as though you were going to write the exam. Try to predict questions that would be found on this type of exam.

When it's time to take the test, follow these steps:

1. Note how much time you have to complete the exam and then give yourself a specific number of minutes per question.

2. Answer the questions you know first. When you do not know the answer to a question, skip it and come back to it later.

3. Look over your exam before handing it in to make sure you have answered all the questions.

Matching Questions

Following are tools you can use when your exam has matching questions.

- **Determine the pattern of the matching questions.** Take a minute before you begin answering questions to determine exactly what is being matched. Are you matching people with quotes, words with definitions, or events with descriptions?

- **Read the longest column first.** One column will probably have more information than the other column. If you begin by reading the column with the most information and matching it to the column with the least amount of reading, you can avoid having to reread the lengthy material.

- **Answer the questions you know first.** If you aren't sure about one of the matching items, come back and match it up later. You may find you have only a match or two left at the end and you can make a decision then. Once again, don't forget to double-check your exam when you are finished to make sure you didn't leave something unmarked or unanswered.

- **As you answer, cross out the items used from both columns.** This timesaver lets you know you have already matched items. This way, you don't have to waste time rereading those items you have already matched.

Essay Question Tools

Essay questions can be fairly easy if you follow the tips in this section. It has several pointers on how to write a successful essay exam. Review these tips often so you become familiar with them.

Essay Exam Preparation Tools

To prepare for essay questions, use the following strategies:

- Memorize key phrases, definitions, or short passages.

- Learn main ideas, key terms, steps, and processes.

- Know the concepts and ideas, not just names and dates.

- Anticipate exam questions. If you have studied different management styles, for example, you would want to be able to compare and contrast those styles.

A Step-by-Step Approach to Answering Essay Questions

For essay questions, we advise you to read the question carefully, brainstorm for creative ideas, and then use those ideas to make an outline before you begin writing. Brainstorm and outline even if the essay test is timed; doing so will make the process easier and quicker in the long run. Learn to allow your first ideas to flow and know you can edit them into a more formal essay later. Do not write for the reader (your instructor) while you are in the creative stage. The more logical your outline, the easier your essay will be to follow and the more likely you will be to get a better score.

Get into the habit of approaching essay questions in a step-by-step fashion. You can follow our step-by-step plan:

> **Note:** Typically essays are written in the third person unless you are talking about yourself or telling someone what to do.

1. Read the question carefully.

   Think: Does it ask for your opinion?

2. Brainstorm ideas or create a mind web, also referred to as a mind map. As you learned in Chapter 1, "Study Skills," a mind web or mind map is a way of graphically organizing your thoughts. The ReadWriteThink.org website offers a tool that can help you create an essay mind map:

   www.readwritethink.org/files/resources/interactives/essaymap

3. Categorize your topic, numbering each category.

   Think: There's an obvious outline for this topic. What is it?

   I.

   II.

   III.

4. Rank and sort your brainstormed ideas into your outline.

   Think: You should have three points of interest (or examples) for each category.

   I.

      A.

      B.

      C.

   II.

      A.

      B.

C.

III.

A.

B.

C.

5. Take a few minutes to rethink the topic from an interesting angle.

6. Make sure that you accomplish these tasks with your introduction:

   • Begin with an attention getter.

   • Segue into your topic.

   • Tell the reader your topic.

   • Tell the reader your outline or the categories that you are going to write about.

   • Include a thesis (position) statement.

7. Begin writing the body of the paper.

   Think: What phrases can transition smoothly from topic to topic? Look at the following example.

   Sample essay question: Supporters of technology say that it solves problems and leads to a higher quality of life. Opponents argue that technology creates new problems that may threaten or harm the quality of life. Discuss these two positions. Which view of technology do you support? Why?

   Transition sentence for Paragraph 2:

   "To begin with, advances in technology have provided many benefits for mankind. For example, …"

Transition sentence for Paragraph 3:

"Although technology has created such advances for modern man, it has also caused many problems and comes at a price to society. An example of how technology can be a detriment is …"

Transition sentence for Paragraph 4 (note the use of the word support, *which came from the question):*

"As has been discussed, technology has positive and negative aspects. After weighing these differences, I tend to *support* the position that technology, when used responsibly, is far better than living without it. One of the reasons I feel this way is because …"

Conclusion:

"In summary, it has been said that nothing in life comes without a price. In the case of technology, this rule also holds true. The price of advanced technology is a tradeoff for the environment, forced community involvement, and sometimes "playing God" in medical advances. This essay has discussed the two positions of technology. There are no easy answers to the gap created by technology. However, I do believe we can continue to become both technologically advanced and ethically responsible without having these options be mutually exclusive…"

8. Proofread your answer before submitting it.

   If you have access to spelling and/or grammar checking tools, use them. If they are not available in the online platform for your class, write your essay in Microsoft Word or even an e-mail and spell check it before you copy and paste it into your essay answer box. Proofreading is important. Even simple things such as the number of spaces after periods and using the proper font and line spacing can improve your overall grade.

Additional Essay Question Tools

Following are other tools that can help you when you take essay exams:

- **Read through the entire exam once before you start writing.** If answers come to mind immediately for some questions, jot down keywords while they are fresh in your mind, but don't start writing until you have read through the exam once.

- **Budget your time.** Allow enough time at the end to go back and finish incomplete answers and to proofread your answers.

- **Answer questions you know first.**

- **Don't panic about any question you think you do not know.** Stay calm. Come back to those. As you relax, you probably will remember the answers to those questions later. Come back and do them last.

- **Take time to structure your answer.** Whenever you can, work from a brief outline jotted down on scratch paper before you begin to write. Select what is clearly relevant; avoid rambling and repetition.

- **Get to the point.** Your first sentence should sum up your main point. If you are writing a lengthy answer, summarize, in an introductory paragraph, the key points you intend to make. If you aren't sure about something, it is better to have less content and get the facts straight instead of pulling together several vague sentences that say the same thing over and over. Professors know all the tricks. You can't trick them into thinking you know the information when you don't.

- **Qualify answers when in doubt.** It is better to say "toward the end of the 20th century" than to say "1990" when you can't remember whether it is 1990 or 1992. The general date may be all that is necessary, but you may lose credit for a specific but incorrect date.

- **Take time at the end to reread the exam.** Make sure you have answered all the questions and have answered all parts of the question.

Keywords in Essay Questions

Professors are very particular about the wording of essay questions and how they should be answered. If an essay question asks you to discuss something and you make a list, for example, you will lose points and could possibly get zero points for your answer.

The following table defines words that are commonly used in essay questions. Become familiar with these words and what is expected from you when you see them in an essay question. Being familiar with the words can make the difference between receiving partial credit and no credit on an answer.

Common Words Used in Essay Questions

Compare	Examine characteristics in order to determine likeness.
Contrast	Stress dissimilarities, differences, or unlikeness of association.
Criticize	Express your judgment with respect to the correctness or merit of the factors under consideration.
Define	Write concise, clear, authoritative meanings. Keep in mind the class to which the item belongs and whatever differentiates it from all other classes.
Discuss	Examine and analyze carefully. Present pros and cons.
Enumerate	A list or outline form of reply–recount, one by one, the points required.
Evaluate	Present an appraisal, stressing advantages and limitations.
Explain	Clarify and interpret the material you present.
Illustrate	Present a figure, diagram, or concrete example.
Interpret	Translate, solve, or comment on the subject. Give a judgment or reaction.
Justify	Prove your thesis or show grounds for your decision.
List	Present an itemized series or tabulation.
Outline	Give main points and supplementary material in a systematic manner.

(continued)

(continued)

Prove	Establish something with certainty by citing evidence or by logical reasoning.
Relate	Emphasize connections and associations.
Review	Emphasize and comment briefly in organized sequence on the major points.
State	Express the main points in a brief, clear way.
Summarize	Give in condensed form the main points or facts.
Trace	Describe the progress, sequence, or development from the point of origin.

Test Anxiety Tools

If you have test anxiety, you don't have to be defeated. You can take action. Most students have some level of stress around an exam, but they can manage it effectively.

First, let's discuss how you can recognize test anxiety. Some students actually get physical distress symptoms such as nausea, headaches, faintness, or feeling overheated or too cold. Other students feel less physical symptoms, but more emotional ones. They want to or even do cry; laugh too much; or feel helpless, angry, or frustrated. Either way, test tension affects their performance. Other students might have panic attacks or hyperventilate. Some students become so tense in the neck and shoulders that they can't get enough blood to their brains, affecting their ability to think well and causing them to blank out or have racing thoughts that are hard to slow down and focus.

If you suffer from major test anxiety, fear not. There is hope. Begin by taking slow, deep breaths, and then read the following sections.

Prepare Physically

Being well prepared for an exam is essential to reducing your stress level. Use the study skills discussed in Chapter 1 to prepare yourself for exams.

Stay healthy by eating nutritious food, exercising, and getting enough sleep. Yes, we know you have heard it all before. The truth is that your body fuels your brain and must be in good shape for mental trials.

Make sure you have all your supplies with you for the exam. It always amazes professors how many students show up on exam day with no test-taking implements in hand. Don't be one of the students who show up for an exam without a pen or pencil. If you need to use a calculator for a math, accounting, or other course, make sure that you take it with you, it works, and the batteries are new. Bring a spare calculator with you just in case yours breaks down. Have a snack handy and some water.

Lessen your stress by knowing when and where your exam is. Many schools have different times set aside for final exams. Double-check the date, time, and place of your exam so that you aren't anxiously hunting for that information on test day.

Prepare Mentally

Thoughts are exercise for your brain. What you think about will expand. If you are living in fear of the exam, it will start consuming you, literally running your life. Use positive thought patterns and messages instead. Your thoughts will eventually create your beliefs, which will in turn result in actions. Change your thoughts, and soon you will start affecting your reactions.

Say these affirmations to yourself:

> "Of course I can do well on this test."

> "I studied, and the answers will come to me."

> "I am a confident test taker."

Repeat these simple affirmations daily until test day. If you freeze up during the test, breathe. And keep doing deep, slow breathing throughout the test.

You can teach yourself to calm down by repeating a calming word, such as "Peace," while you are taking the exam. This word can work as a trigger for your mind. You can take some deep, slow breaths and keep saying the trigger word throughout the exam. If needed, stop, stretch, breathe, and say, "I will do fine. I know this material. I will do well."

Note: If you feel that your test anxiety is unmanageable, consider working with someone who does energy work (such as Reiki) around panic. For severe or prolonged anxiety, consult a psychologist or other mental health professional.

Then go back to your test.

You have learned the habit of being stressed for an exam, and it will take a bit of undoing to get a new habit around test taking, but you can! That is the good news. You are not the first one to have text anxiety. Others have moved to a new place beyond it, and so can you! Believe in yourself and stop comparing your insides to other's outsides. Stay positive and be well prepared.

For those with substantial test anxiety, we recommend the following test anxiety tools.

Overcome Test Anxiety

Follow this checklist to overcome test anxiety:

- ❑ Know in advance when the tests and quizzes are and how much they are weighted toward your total points for the course.

- ❑ From the beginning of the course, ask about the midterm and final exams so you can plan for them. Work backward from test date to set a study schedule so that you will be ready when test time comes.

- ❑ Find out what format the test is in: essay, true/false, multiple choice, and so on.

- ❑ Be present for the midterm and final reviews if they are available. Your presence is essential in order to understand what is most likely going to be tested.

- ❑ Study in the way that is successful for you. If cramming is successful and you enjoy it, then cram. If cramming does not work for you (and it does not work for many students, although they continue to use it anyway), study 15 to 30 minutes a day instead of three hours the night before.

- ❑ Guess what the instructor might test you on and ask for test study tips. Most instructors will give them to you.

- ❑ Commit important concepts to memory.

❑ Give your brain at least one hour to rest before the exam.

❑ Eat before the test—something with protein to sustain you, but not a lot of carbs (they will give you a quick sugar rush but then make you sleepy).

❑ Prepare mentally to take the test by breathing deeply and visualizing a positive outcome, a perfect grade.

❑ Before you take the test, think of something that relaxes you and the sweet victory you will feel after you ace the test!

❑ Read the directions on the test twice before beginning.

❑ Read all the questions on the test before you start. This allows your subconscious to start solving some questions as you are working on others.

❑ Use the process of elimination. If you do not know the correct answer on a multiple-choice question, try to figure it out by crossing out the answers that you are certain are wrong.

❑ If you are not sure, guess. Statistically speaking, random guessing won't hurt you.

❑ Do not cross out any answers in a test unless you are certain they are wrong.

❑ If you get stuck on a question, make a note in the margin and move on, letting your subconscious work on the problem you are stuck on.

❑ Go at your own pace.

❑ Eliminate negative statements about yourself.

❑ Think of quirky and funny ways to remember information. Approaching tests with a sense of humor reduces anxiety and can improve your performance. In other words, try to get yourself to lighten up mentally. The test is a big deal, but you are a bigger deal and can handle it.

❑ If you have a brain freeze, stop, take a deep breath, and count to 10. Tell yourself you know the answers, and they are coming to you easily. Keep breathing. Then go to the next question.

❑ Realize that you know what you know and keep moving forward.

❑ Give yourself a reward when the test is over.

❑ Use the test results to study for future tests.

❑ Go back and figure out why you got an answer wrong. Question your instructor if you don't understand why you got it wrong. Explain your logic; you might get more points by doing so.

Some of these checkpoints may sound familiar. Remember this: If you see something more than once, you have a better chance of remembering it.

Conclusion

Students suffer from test-taking anxiety for a variety of reasons. The main reason is not being well prepared for an exam. Other reasons students suffer from test anxiety are worries they have about past performance, how well others are doing, and the negative consequences they face if they fail. Reading this chapter and using the tools provided should alleviate most or all of your test anxiety, especially anxiety concerning being well prepared. You will alleviate other anxieties by continuing to build your self-confidence when you read the chapters on attitude and motivation that are coming up.

Best Practices: Test-Taking Skills

Do

- Do use the study skills you learned in Chapter 1.

- Do listen in class for hints about what might be on the exam.

- Do study for your exam.

- Do learn the tools for the different types of test questions.

- Do practice test-taking skills. Develop templates for answering essay-type questions in an outline format.

- Do pay close attention to and know what the words that are often used in essay questions mean.

- Do learn how to overcome test anxiety. It will help your test performance and overall grade.

Don't

- Don't study at the last minute, trying to cram for exams. Your body and mind need rest and care if they are to function well.

- Don't worry about how others are doing, your past performance, or negative thoughts about failure.

- Don't let test anxiety rule you. Test taking is a learned skill. The more confident you become in your skill, the less anxiety you will have.

Assignment 2.1: Learn About Test Anxiety

In this assignment, you explore a website to learn more about test anxiety. Go to the following website and answer the questions about its content:

http://ub-counseling.buffalo.edu/stresstestanxiety

1. What are six physical symptoms of test anxiety?

_____

_____

_____

_____

_____

_____

2. What are the effects of test anxiety?

_____

_____

_____

(continued)

(continued)

3. What are five things you can do to reduce test anxiety?

_____

_____

_____

_____

_____

Assignment 2.2: Practice Test-Taking Skills

In this assignment, implement the suggestions in this chapter.

1. Find out the format of the test and what might be on the exam.

2. Review the test-taking tips for that format.

3. Go to YouTube and watch videos on test-taking strategies. The following are some helpful links. If you can't find the links, just go to YouTube and type in "test taking strategies," and you will see a listing of several helpful videos.

Professor Nightengale's Test-Taking Strategies for Nursing Students (www.professornightengale.com):

www.youtube.com/watch?v=Gc5L3SmPs4Q

The following videos are part of a series produced by Paul Devoto and featuring teachers from the Jonas Salk High-Tech Academy in Sacramento, California:

Test-Taking Strategies 1—Eliminating Wrong Answers:

www.youtube.com/watch?v=l0P5U9s4wYE

Test-Taking Strategies 2—Working Backwards:

www.youtube.com/watch?v=vEF_mkeFawU

Test-Taking Strategies 3—Solving Easy Problems First:

www.youtube.com/watch?v=4XYMkBib9Cw

Test-Taking Strategies 4—Staying Relaxed:

www.youtube.com/watch?v=bvQHk9WUjKg

Test-Taking Strategies 5—The Secret Spill:

www.youtube.com/watch?v=f5YjVNgWjpU

Test-Taking Strategies 6—Show Your Work:

www.youtube.com/watch?v=PSmycb0b9yo

These are just a few of the videos online these days that can help you with study skills or test-taking skills. Don't be afraid to go out and search for them.

4. Take notes if the professor has a test review. Tape the test review if possible.

5. Review the chapters you have read and your notes. Pay special attention to the items gone over during the test review.

6. Get some rest the night before the test. Eat breakfast.

7. Show up early for the exam. Review your notes.

8. Do some relaxation exercises before the exam. Remember that you are well prepared and should do well on your exam.

9. When you receive the results of your exam, note how much better you did compared to what you have done on previous exams.

CHAPTER 3

Perception, Learning Styles, and Personality

"Preconceived notions are the locks on the door to wisdom."

Merry Browne

We all go through life being told how we are and why we do the things we do. These preconceived ideas can keep us from being successful. In this chapter, we look at how identifying your learning style and personality type can change how you see yourself. This chapter also shows you how not knowing these two things can affect your academic success. By the end of this chapter, you will come to understand how knowing yourself better and getting rid of some of those preconceived notions you have about yourself can help you on your road to success.

Perception

Your perception of yourself comes from conditioning, from statements you have heard over and over again throughout your life. You learn "how you are" (that is, that you are not good at math or that you are clumsy) from parents, family, friends, teachers, and acquaintances. After the perception of "how you are" is firmly in your subconscious, it stays there until the perception is changed.

For example, you may have heard that you are not good at math. Your parents have told you, teachers have told you, your spouse may have told you, and you may have told yourself. You have been told that you are not good at math so many times you finally believe it.

People act not in accordance with the truth, but with what they believe the truth to be. This is how an inaccurate or uninformed perception and self-concept can sabotage your success. What if the reason for your not doing well in math is that your teacher used a teaching style that was not effective with your learning style? What if you had no idea you even had a learning style and were studying in the wrong way? The question then becomes this: Is it that you are not good at math or that you have never used your learning style properly to process mathematical information?

The way to answer these questions and challenge your perceptions of yourself is to spend time truly evaluating "how you are," starting with your learning style.

Learning Styles

A learning style can be defined as how you take in information, process it, and learn it. To better understand what your learning style is, you will want to take a learning style assessment, sometimes referred to as an inventory.

Don't let the word *assessment* scare you. It isn't a test or an exam. It is just a tool used to find out information about you. Many people find the accuracy of assessments amazing.

To find out more about your learning style, complete Assignment 3.1 in this chapter and then read the sections on the three basic learning styles—visual, auditory, and kinesthetic/tactile—and study tips for each learning style. Knowing your learning style may give you a slightly different perception of yourself.

When you are taking the assessment, you should

- **Read each statement carefully.**

- **Choose the statement that comes closest to stating how you act and behave *most* of the time.** Take your time, read the statements carefully, and answer honestly so that your results will be more accurate. If you just mark items without thinking about them, the results will not be valid. A student once took the assessment, marking everything the opposite of the truth. The results showed that this person was extremely outgoing. In reality, he was extremely shy and quiet. He was called on in class many times because the instructor saw from the assessment that he was more outgoing than others. The student was very uncomfortable and finally confessed that he had cheated on the assessment. He was glad to get back into his comfort zone and not be called on in class as often.

- **If you do not understand a word, look it up in the dictionary.** Misunderstanding the meaning of a word can make a difference in the results of the assessment. People will not think you are stupid if you look up words. They probably will be relieved to see someone else doesn't know a word, and they will not feel bad about using a dictionary. Be a leader; don't follow the herd.

Remember this general rule when looking at your test results: these results will not match you exactly. The test is only a tool to give you a clearer picture of yourself. However, if you answered the questions honestly, you probably will be surprised at how accurate the results are. You might even change some self-perceptions that have been holding you back.

Assignment 3.1: Find Your Learning Style

In this assignment, you complete a short, easy learning style assessment. It can give you a basic awareness of your learning style.

1. Go to this website to access the Diablo Valley College Learning Style Survey (written by Catherine Jester):

   www.metamath.com/lsweb/dvclearn.htm

2. Click on Learning Styles Survey to begin the learning styles inventory.

3. For accurate results, answer the questions honestly and "like you are most of the time."

4. Save and print your results to share with the class.

Visual Learners

If your highest number scored is for visual learning, you are considered to be a visual learner. Approximately 40 percent of learners are visual learners, who learn best by seeing and picturing. Visual learners learn best either verbally or nonverbally.

Visual verbal learners prefer to read to learn information instead of listening to a lecture or a discussion. They prefer seeing written instructions as well as hearing them. These learners make lists regularly of daily goals and activities. A visual verbal learner would prefer watching documentaries and films where both visual and verbal information is being presented.

Videos, diagrams, and demonstrations are excellent ways for a visual nonverbal learner to learn new material. When browsing reading material, these learners focus on pictures, charts, and maps. This type of learner enjoys learning through observation, preferring demonstrations over written materials and watching videos over listening to lectures. Visual nonverbal learners would rather watch the news than read the news.

If you are a visual learner, you probably

- Make vivid and detailed movies in your mind about what you are reading.

- Pay close attention to the body language and facial expressions of others.

- Are well organized and neat.

- Have a keen awareness of your environment and use image and color to increase retention of information.

You can make the most of your visual learning style by using these study tips:

- Look for videos to supplement the subject you are learning.

- Read your text before you go to class. Spend time looking at the diagrams and examples.

- Highlight and underline key terms and concepts in your notes and books. Use different colors of pens and markers to take notes and to highlight your books.

- Look up words you do not understand. Buy an inexpensive dictionary and keep it with you for this purpose.

Auditory Learners

If your highest score is in the auditory section, you are an auditory learner. In other words, you learn best by listening. Approximately 30 percent of learners are auditory. An auditory learner prefers lectures and understands verbal directions well.

If you are an auditory learner, you probably

- Learn well through verbal explanations.

- Enjoy class discussion and taking part or watching role-playing.

- Are distracted easily by noise but tend to remember information when it is associated with sounds.

- Need more time to process information and to ask questions.

- Talk through problems.

- Learn by listening, repeating, and planning aloud.

These study tips work well for auditory learners:

- Record class lectures and test reviews as a helpful study aid.

- Start a study group and listen carefully to others who attend the study group session.

- Review information by listening to recordings, and then repeating the information you need to know.

Kinesthetic/Tactile Learners

If you scored highest in the kinesthetic/tactile area, you are in a group that makes up approximately 15 percent of all learners. Put simply, kinesthetic/tactile learners learn best by doing. Hands-on experience and physical activity are the best methods to use with these learners. They like to be physically involved in the learning environment.

If you are a kinesthetic/tactile learner, you probably

- Learn well in a lab setting. For example, you learn computer skills best by actually using the computer.

- Learn concepts by applying them.

- Like to do group projects.

- Will try to put something together without reading directions.
- Have trouble sitting still for long periods.

Use these study tips if you are a kinesthetic/tactile learner:

- Do not do the assignment only once; repeat it several times. If you are doing accounting problems or exercises, for example, do them a few times.
- Read ahead, using your finger to follow along for better concentration.
- Write questions to ask during lecture.
- Work on one subject at a time until it is finished.
- Make a list of topics to study.
- Break the material you need to learn into smaller increments, studying in chunks instead of all at once.
- Take frequent breaks when studying. If you don't, you can easily be distracted and might have trouble sitting still.
- Plan on studying for several sessions before a test.
- Study in the morning—that's when you're more apt to do your best.

Can you have more than one learning style? Yes. The numbers on your score may show that you are very close in two areas or that you are fairly even in all three styles. Those are good results because they show that you are flexible and can learn in more than one way. You are likely to adjust easily to different teaching styles professors may have.

The learning style assessment you took was a very straightforward, simple one. More complex assessments are available. If you find the topic of learning styles interesting and want to learn more about it, check out the information in the appendix at the end of this book. It lists several books and websites where you can go to learn more about your learning style.

You can also return to the site where you took your assessment:

www.metamath.com/lsweb/dvclearn.htm

Click on the Learning Styles and Strategies link to learn more about the results of your learning styles assessment.

Sources for Additional Help

When you discover your learning style and use the appropriate study tips, you will be on your way to becoming a more successful student. However, if you continue to have problems understanding the material in a difficult class, you may want to see an academic coach or tutor.

If your university or school does not offer an academic coach or tutor service, you may find some of the following suggestions useful:

- Ask classmates or friends to clarify something you don't understand. They may be able to explain it to you in a way that will help you understand the material.

- Get together with other students in your class and start a study group or schedule a study session once a week.

- Look for additional materials on the subject at your campus or public library. Libraries sometimes have videos and audio recordings in the subjects you are studying that can help you.

Online Learners and Learning Styles

Visual learners and kinesthetic learners do quite well in the online environment. The fact that students use the keyboard and their brain especially helps with the tactile/kinesthetic learners. Much online education is geared toward these two learning styles, but this is beginning to change. Many schools are adding video, audio, and live seminars.

If you are an auditory learner who is taking an online class, just make sure you discuss what you are learning: Verbalize it to others (and yourself). You might also look for YouTube videos that cover the topic you are learning to help you.

Personality Assessment

Personalities are like opinions; everyone has one. Your *personality* is the combination of all your behavioral and emotional traits. Finding out your personality type gives you a clearer picture of who you are.

Earlier, we discussed perception and its effect on your success. We talked about how you may have sabotaged your academic success by listening to someone tell you that you aren't good at math. You may also have been conditioned about other personal traits. You may have been told that you are shy or clumsy. However, one of the greatest misperceptions people can have is a misperception about their personality.

You may believe that you are shy when in reality you could just be a quiet person. Or you may believe that you are stubborn. Some people are proud that they are stubborn. They say that it is in their genes to be stubborn. In reality, stubbornness is a personality trait that could be sabotaging you in many ways—one of which is to keep you from having an open mind toward learning new things.

A personality assessment can reveal another piece of the puzzle as to who you are and the perception that you have of yourself. Several personality assessments are available. In the following sections, you will have the opportunity to take a couple of assessments and learn how they can help you succeed.

The Jung Typology Test

In Assignment 3.2, you take the Jung Typology Test. This test is based on the Keirsey Personality Assessment and has more than 70 questions. Consequently, it takes some time to complete it. Please complete this assignment before you finish reading this chapter.

When you finish taking and scoring your assessment, you will get a four-letter personality type. You can go to the websites shown on your results page to read about the four-letter personality type you have.

The assessment will also give you some ideas about certain traits you may want to change. If you find that you are assessed as being extremely introverted, for example, you may want to work on being more outgoing. Doing so could improve your career as well as your performance as a student.

Assignment 3.2: Take the Jung Typology Test

In this assignment, you complete a personality assessment that takes some effort. The reward is that the results can give you a basic awareness of your personality type.

1. Go to the HumanMetrics website to access the Jung Typology Test:

   www.humanmetrics.com/cgi-win/JTypes2.asp

2. Read through the statements slowly and mark either Yes or No to describe how you are most of the time.

3. After completing the assessment, click on the Score It button for a score.

4. Follow these directions carefully: After getting your score, you will see "Your Type Is" and then a four-letter sequence. You may see results that show you are an INFP or an IESJ or another four-letter type. You want to look for that four-letter sequence. This is your four-letter personality type.

5. Print this page. You will also be printing two other pages.

6. Look for two lines under your four-letter personality type. Those are links to other pages.

7. Click on the first type description link (it should take you to Keirsey.com) and print the page that appears, the portrait (description) of your personality type.

8. Go back to your results page and click on the next type description link (it should take you to the TypeLogic website), a profile of your personality type.

9. Print the profile. The three printed pages explain your personality type.

10. Save your printouts to share with your class.

11. Click on other links on the website to access additional information if you would like to read more on personalities.

The 16 personality types are

ESFP	ESFJ	ENFJ	ENTJ
ESTP	ESTJ	ENFP	ENTP

ISFP	ISFJ	INFJ	INTJ
ISTP	ISTJ	INFP	INTP

The following table describes the meaning of the letters used in the personality assessment.

Keirsey's 16 Personality Types

First Letter

E for Extrovert (75% of the population)	I for Introvert (25% of the population)
Are outgoing	Are reserved
Are approachable	Are intense
Talk first, think later	Listen more than talk
Like to socialize	Enjoy quiet
Are drained by reflective thinking	Reflect before acting
Have many friends but know few well	Have few close friends but know them well
Draw energy from social activities	Tend to be drained by social activities

Second Letter

N for Intuition (25% of the population)	S for Sensing (75% of the population)
Like the unknown	Like facts
Like originality	Are down-to-earth
Fantasize	Are realistic and practical
Have a vivid imagination	Focus on what is in front of you

Third Letter

T for Thinking (50% of the population)	F for Feeling (50% of the population)
Are objective	Are subjective
Stand firm	Can be persuaded
Are impersonal	Are personal
Are justice oriented	Are humane
Categorize according to standards	Strive for harmony
Criticize and analyze	Appreciate
Think logically	Express sympathy
Are principle oriented	Make decisions based on values
Use laws to make decisions	Consider extenuating circumstances

Fourth Letter

J for Judgment (50% of the population)	P for Perception (50% of the population)
Plan ahead	Adapt as you go
Settle on a course of action	Believe something will turn up
Make decisions	Gather data
Seek closure	Keep options open
Complete tasks	Hunt treasure
Are certain and determined	Are tentative and emergent
Focus on deadlines	Let life happen
Want to get the show on the road	Prefer to wait and see
Have sense of urgency	Feel that there's plenty of time

Understand that the test results may not be exact; but if you marked the statement stating how you are most of the time, they will be close. Also, remember everything is on a scale. You can be anywhere from 0 to 100 percent on that scale. If you are an I (Introvert), for example, you can be anywhere from extremely introverted to just a little introverted. If you have always thought you are an extrovert but your results are "I" for introvert, you are probably on the lower end of the introvert scale and close to the extrovert side.

Can personalities change? Sure they can. Age is one factor. You will find that the older people get, the less introverted they may become. Education is another factor in changing personalities. Someone who was extremely shy and introverted at one time may have taken some classes on how to be more outgoing. The assessments this person takes after learning how to be more outgoing will show different results.

Why take an assessment? Knowing your personality type will help you understand yourself better and in a more positive way, actually increasing your self-esteem. If you want to become more outgoing, for example, you can read self-help books on that subject. If you want to improve your logic or analytical skills, you can study methods of thinking.

Knowing your personality type can help you in the corporate world as well. Many companies give their employees personality assessments and occupational personality assessments to see which jobs they are best suited for and what areas they should be working in.

Also, most assessments list famous people who have the same personality type as you do, which is fun to know. For additional information on personality types, go to the following websites:

http://typelogic.com

www.humanmetrics.com

Color-Based Personality Assessments

Another assessment that is quick to take (no more than five minutes), fun, and revealing is the Lüscher Color Test. Dr. Max Lüscher studied color psychology, which is the study of how color affects behavior. He found that certain colors cause an emotional response in people. The test itself is based on his findings.

This test can reveal both short-term and long-term personality characteristics and is affected by your emotional state at the time of the test. If you are feeling down or depressed and take the test, those emotions might be reflected in your results. They vary each time you take the test, so the validity is not specific, but it is accurate.

The results describe your existing situation, stress sources, restrained characteristics, desired objective, and actual problem areas. When we have people take this color test in our classes, they are amazed at the accuracy of the results. They think it is fun and gives them a little bit of insight into their current situations.

Although the Lüscher Color Test is used in European countries and overseas, the United States has few experts on this test, though some corporations use it as part of the hiring process. You can find the Lüscher Color Test at this website:

www.colorquiz.com

Many corporations and companies today give their workers color personality assessments. There are several online, and they assess your personality type as well as your behavioral style. Understanding your behavioral style can lead to better communications with others in your professional life, academic life, and personal life.

By taking this type of assessment, you learn what color represents you. Will it be blue for compassionate, gold for responsible, orange for spontaneous, or green for conceptual? Your results indicate what your strongest color is and what your secondary color is. Color assessments can provide insight into your communication and relationship preferences and are another way to let you see why you do the things you do.

You can find a color personality assessment at author Carolyn Kalil's website:

www.truecolorscareer.com/quiz.asp

Other Assessments

Several other assessments are available to help you know yourself better. In high school, for example, you probably took an occupational personality assessment. That type of assessment is scored, and the results list professions suited to your personality type, based on the traits, characteristics, and skills you believe you have. Other occupational assessments frequently given are the *Transition-to-Work Inventory* by Dr. John Liptak and SIGI[3], which creates a list of occupations based on your values, interests, and work skills. Another assessment in this area is the Occupational Personality Questionnaire (OPQ) that is designed to provide information on the typical behavior of an individual within work situations.

Some of the questions these assessments answer are as follows:

- Can you work well with others?
- Do you enjoy being around people?
- Can you solve problems and assess difficult situations?

Administrators find that using these assessments helps them decide which people they should choose for specific jobs. If an assessment such as *Self-Directed Search* by John Holland shows that you are extremely introverted, you may be best suited for a job with little contact with other people.

About.com's Career Planning section provides an overview of assessments in this area and some links to online assessments:

http://careerplanning.about.com/cs/selfassessment

Conclusion

This chapter gave you methods of gaining insight into who you really are. After reading this chapter and completing the assessments, you should know yourself much better. Understanding yourself can reduce preconceived self-perceptions that may not be true. Also, it is fun to find out "how" you really are.

Now that you know your learning style, you can choose the correct way to study. If you have more than one learning style, you can even be more successful with your studies because you have even more tools to use.

Best Practices: Perception, Learning Styles, and Personality

Do

- Do understand how your perceptions can keep you from being successful.
- Do take learning style and personality assessments.
- Do be honest in marking your assessments.
- Do mark your assessments in terms of how you are most of the time.
- Do read the results of your assessments with an open mind.
- Do peruse some additional readings on personality and learning styles.
- Do get to know yourself better.

Don't

- Don't let others tell you how or who you are. Be your own person.
- Don't let others tell you where you want to be and what you want to do.
- Don't mark your answers on assessments in terms of how you "want to be."

CHAPTER 4

Organization

"We have become a society of dilly-dallyers."

Brian Bergman (from the article "Guilt-Free
Goofing Off" in *Maclean's* magazine)

Like most students, you probably have too much on your plate.
Yet consider this interesting saying: "If you want something done,
ask the busiest person you know to do it." In other words, productive
people are often the most organized.

The truth of this saying most likely will become more evident after you
learn the organization strategies and do the assignments in this chapter. If you feel that you are lacking in these skills, fear not—you can
learn them. And keep in mind that with a little practice, a new
behavior can become a habit in about 21 days.

Start with Your Location

Choose a good location to study. Make it one that

- Is conducive to focusing because it is free of noise and clutter.

- Suits your learning style.

- Isn't too comfortable (in other words, not on the couch or curled
  up on a bed).

When you choose a location for studying that lets you be productive, you give your work the respect and importance it deserves. However, no matter how carefully you choose your location, you're likely to run into problems. Here are our problem-solving tips:

- Take notes while you study so that you tune out distractions and stay focused.

- Minimize distractions by turning off the TV or getting earplugs.

- Let voice mail or the answering machine handle phone calls. You would not answer your cell phone in any class (we hope), so why not let the answering machine take (or at least screen) your calls while you are studying?

- If you have too many distractions in your room or at home, go to the library. It's usually a fairly quiet study environment.

- Clean your space. Declutter and don't be afraid to throw things away so you have space and breathing room to work.

Monitor Your Schedule

Organize and monitor study sessions to get the most out of each one. To do that, apply these suggestions:

- Start your assignments early so you can have extra (flex) time in case something unexpected comes along or if you get stuck at some difficult point. This *flex time* will be your saving grace at some point in your college experience. To gain even more flex time, schedule more work for the first half of each course week rather than the latter half.

- Make yourself familiar with the routine of the lessons. Successful students advise you to read each assignment first and glance through the rest of the material, so you know what is coming down the pike.

- Match your work to your energy level, if possible. If your energy is low, you will likely find coursework more enjoyable if you do the easy parts first. That way you will accomplish more in a shorter period of time. Dig into tougher assignments when your energy is at its peak.

- Pay attention to the details. Know in advance when the assignments are going to be due and how much they are weighted toward your total points.

- Make certain that all your assignments, tests, and quizzes are completed by the designated due date. The instructor does not get paid less or more whether you pass or fail the course.

- Create a plan for completing each assignment. Because most instructors take points off for late work, find out what your instructor's policy is, know the due date for the assignment, and plan backward from there so that you know the steps you need to take and the dates you need to complete them. That way you'll stay on target.

- Check your work.

- After you turn in your work, check your grades and answers to make sure you are on the right track.

- Review what you did the previous week before continuing to the next week in order to refresh your memory of what you have covered and to tie it to what you will be learning. Keep in mind that you must review or see new material eight times before your brain crystallizes it.

Organize Logistically

Organizing logistically means mapping out a study plan for a class that is time efficient. You apply this same principle when you are taking a trip. If you are traveling from New York City to Los Angeles, for example, it is most time efficient to travel the straightest line possible. You usually would not want to go to Kentucky and backtrack to Maine, and then head to Ohio, down to Texas, and back to Missouri. Getting to Los Angeles would take you forever!

The logistical organization of your studying should be no different. Simply make a plan of the most practical way for you to navigate the course content. Some students advocate logistically organizing those course items that are the highest priority in the class first. These are most often quizzes, tests, and assignments. For example, put all assignments, quizzes, and tests on a calendar so you know what is coming up and can prepare for them in advance. Whatever logistical method you choose to get through your class, make sure that you don't miss any stops along the way.

After you have spent some time in the class, determine whether you have the most efficient and effective logistical map. Predict the amount of time you need to do your assignments and then see if you can beat that time! We are not giving you permission to rush to the point that you do shabby work—we're suggesting that you try to work effectively and efficiently without being sloppy. Predicting and monitoring your time spent on assignments will give you an indication of how organized you are.

If you develop a plan and stick to it, the time you spend studying for class should be reduced, assuming that you have a similar workload from week to week. When you reduce your studying time, your logistical organization plan is working. However, if your number of assignments increases, you will need to revamp your organizational plan.

Assignment 4.1: Create a Logistical Plan

For this assignment, you make a simple plan of what you need to do for class.

1. List all the assignments you have and when exams are coming up. Consider putting them on a month-at-a-glance calendar.

2. Rate your assignments from most to least important.

3. Make a plan for your high-priority assignments first. Choose a method of going through your prioritized list—from top to bottom, or left to right, or a combination that works for you. Make a plan for everything you need to do for that class.

4. Organize your plan into a daily or weekly schedule.

5. Try out your completed plan.

6. Keep a record of how long it takes you to finish assignments for classes you have organized and those you don't have organized. Assuming similar workloads, your study time for the organized classes should decrease as you become more proficient in managing your time and adept at following your organizational plan.

7. Be prepared to share your plan with the class.

Learn Additional Organization Secrets from Successful Students

We polled some successful students for strategies they use to keep themselves organized. Their tips include the following:

- Do your assignments early in the week. If something comes up later in the week, you will already have your course work completed, and you'll have one less thing to worry about.

- Plan ahead so that you can complete your large projects early and review them before you submit them.

- Spend a little time each day reading your assignments. This will help you concentrate on what you are reading so you are focusing on the material you need for your assignments. Otherwise, you will most likely miss half or more of what you read.

- Spend some time each day reviewing your assignment requirements. Otherwise, you will most likely miss important parts of the assignments.

- Time yourself when you read. See how long it takes you to read 5 to 10 pages so that you can accurately estimate how long you need for your study sessions.

- Do extra research on the tough assignments, using the library or resources that are available online.

- Don't overwork.

- Set a stopping time, forcing yourself to work in a more focused manner. Then reward yourself for doing some work.

Handle Special Organizational Situations

Students do not all enter college at the same time of life. Nor do all students attend class on campus. This section shares organizational tips for two special situations: students who have families to care for and online students.

Organize Around Families

If you have family members to take care of, you may need to organize your studying around caring for them. Here are some suggestions:

- Make a balanced, win-win plan with your family for your study time so that they have a reason to give you the space and time you need. In other words, negotiate a "reward" for giving you study time.

- Set a timer and then do what you said you would do.

- If you are studying and have small children, take frequent breaks and make certain the children have good things to occupy their time.

- Arrange a co-op with another parent. You can take turns swapping study time for child care.

- Know your limits and be realistic about your course load. Take a little longer to finish your degree so that you are able to have a nicer journey along the way.

One successful student we know organizes toys, snacks, and a movie for his children to keep them content while he studies. They all plan an activity they will do together when he takes a break. He is always thinking "win-win."

Organize for Online Learning

So what are the secret pearls of wisdom other successful online students offer for organization? Here is what they say:

- Most online classes have some type of orientation. Make sure you complete it when you start the class, even if doing so is optional.

- Most online classes have some type of "Start Here" section when you start the class. Pay attention to it. This section can make or break you because it shows you how to easily navigate online.

- Find the syllabus right away, print it, and use it as your guide for deadlines. Map all deadlines on your calendar, so you can see them coming up. Consider color coding each class so you can differentiate those class assignments easily. Put a red star or mark on the day in the calendar where there is a test or major project due. This allows you time to prepare.

- Every day when you first log on, go through your new e-mail messages, check grades, and check the discussion board before you begin the next segment.

- Stay with the assigned schedule or work ahead if it is allowed.

- Make sure you take part in any scheduled chat room discussion and post to the class online discussion board. These areas make the course more fun and usually are graded.

- Find out what the minimum number of discussion posts are that you need each week, how long they need to be, and what day of the week they need to be submitted. Plot this on your calendar as a reminder. Also find out any other details, such as whether the instructor needs the discussion posts to be referenced or in APA style (see Chapter 8, "Research Paper Writing").

- Print the more challenging assignments and have them handy so you can think about them for a couple of days. Soon they will be familiar and not look so hard anymore.

- Break the more difficult assignments into smaller pieces.

- Don't assume that you know it all and skim through the material. Let the work sink into you.

- Do all your assignments and take enough time to make them meaningful.

- Logistically organize online work, based on proximity, so you don't forget anything. If the grade book is left of the online discussion tab, for example, some students check the grade book first and then go to the online discussion tab.

- Develop an organizational pattern in the class and follow it step by step. If you do the steps in the order set forth, the assignments will most likely build on each other, and it is less likely that you will forget one.

- Use the 5-Minute Rule: If you have five minutes, you have time, so jump into your class and read or write in the discussions or check your e-mail messages.

- If your online class gives you a checklist for each chapter or unit, print the list and cross off the items when you have them completed. See the sample daily/weekly checklist that follows.

Each day check

- ❑ Class e-mail
- ❑ Announcement center
- ❑ Weekly assignments
- ❑ For quizzes or tests
- ❑ Discussion board
- ❑ Turned-in assignments in the drop box
- ❑ Grade book
- ❑ Document-sharing area and/or online library
- ❑ Course objectives
- ❑ Big project status (in other words, term projects or papers)
- ❑ Weekly online lecture material
- ❑ Online chat room scheduled discussions

Conclusion

Just as you plan your vacation or your future, you need to plan and organize your classes in order to succeed. If you try to succeed without an organized plan, we guarantee you will miss something. Planning will get you the results you want—within a shorter time span.

Do you remember Murphy's Laws? Yes, more than one Murphy's Law exists. Here are just a few:

Nothing is as easy as it looks.

Everything takes longer than you think it will. Plan for that.

Anything that can go wrong will go wrong. Have a plan B and C!

If anything simply can't go wrong, it will anyway.

Left to themselves, things tend to go from bad to worse.

If you want to read more on Murphy's Laws, go to this website:

www.murphys-laws.com/murphy/murphy-true.html

Being well-prepared requires that we each take the responsibility for our own success. Even though we would like to and sometimes do lean on others, we are responsible. If you practice the organizational strategies in this chapter frequently, they will become habits, and your potential will be unleashed.

Best Practices: Organization

Do

- Do organize your workspace. Knowing where your equipment is optimizes your time.

- Do limit your distractions. Plan ahead to determine when and where you will find the quietest location.

- Do balance your life. Take time for family, friends, hobbies, and so on. Doing so will make you more efficient and effective. Make it win-win! Others have done this and so can you!

- Do develop a logistical plan for studying. (For online students, decide whether you will go to the discussion area first; then check e-mail, grades, assignments, and so on.) You should stick to the plan unless your time efficiency drops.

- Do organize your assignments. Begin them early in the week so you have flex time that may be needed later in the week.

- Do choose to do easy or hard assignments first depending on your energy level. If your energy is high, successful students usually choose to do the hard assignments first.

- Do use the 5-Minute Rule to get things done in class when you feel you have no time.

- Do use a checklist. Whether you print the syllabus or a formal class checklist, keep it handy and mark off the tasks as you complete them each week.

Don't

- Don't minimize the importance of an organized plan. If you do, you will waste time and perform below your potential.

- Don't overorganize your life. Some people spend too much time developing a time management strategy and never do anything. Overorganizing is counterproductive. Just get an organizational plan together, stick to it, and tweak it only if needed. Don't become obsessive with organizing.

(continued)

(continued)

- Don't let yourself become overwhelmed. If you do, you will freeze up and be unable to accomplish anything effectively or efficiently.

Assignment 4.2: Organize Your Week

For this assignment, you organize your assignments for one week.

1. Make a list of assignments that are due for that week to organize yourself.

2. Write down what you need to do for each assignment to finish it.

3. Check off each assignment as you finish it, making a note to yourself of whether studying went better because you were organized and knew that you were staying on top of things.

4. Save your checklist to share with the class.

CHAPTER 5

Attitude

*"You are never given a wish without also
being given the power to make it come true.
You may have to work for it, however."*

Richard Bach

Have you asked yourself why you are pursuing a college degree? If the answer is anything other than "I want to," then you are not ready to dive in headfirst. If you would rather be doing other things, you will be distracted from your studies and will likely quit. Once you set your *why* for getting a degree, you then focus on that *why* often. The fuel for getting the job done (graduating) comes with the *why* not the *how*. If you keep focusing on *how* you will be able to do it, you will likely lose your momentum. Successful students focus on the *why* and a mental picture of the end result: their diplomas!

When you focus on being a student and getting your degree, the rest falls into place. A positive attitude is the spark that starts you on the road to your goal. Attitude breeds commitment. Commitment leads to motivation. Motivation leads to success. These things are all interrelated and are essential to your success.

Realize That Input Equals Output

You get out of your classes exactly what you put into them. If your attitude toward education is positive, you will receive a positive experience and education. However, if your attitude is negative, you will have a negative experience and education. As with most things in life, you get to decide. It's all up to you and your attitude.

Nike uses the famous slogan "Just Do It" in its advertising. In the "Anyway" poem made famous by Mother Teresa (and based on "The Paradoxical Commandments" by Dr. Kent M. Keith), readers are encouraged to keep taking action and trying even when the obstacles are large and the outcome is uncertain. These principles are appropriately linked to education:

- Getting a degree is a difficult task. Do it anyway.

- Getting a degree requires time management and organizational skills. Do it anyway.

- Participating in some classes requires you to have specific computer skills. Do it anyway.

- You may not want to or feel that you need to take a required class. Do it anyway.

- You may prefer to go to a party or a movie with friends instead of studying. Do it (study) anyway.

The premise here, of course, is that you must adopt an attitude of empowerment and ability. Despite the fact that you might have other things you would rather do than go to class and participate, do it anyway and tell yourself you want to. This class won't last forever, and getting a degree is worth the extra effort now. Remind yourself that your effort will pay off!

You lean in the direction you feel strongly about. If you want that degree, keep affirming to yourself, "I can do this." If you say that to yourself often enough and really want it, you will do it.

If you have a positive attitude, you will lean toward the positive outcome. If you have a negative attitude, you will make up all kinds of reasons not to accomplish your goal.

There are only two reasons people do not accomplish their goals:

- They *don't* want it badly enough.

- They *can't* see themselves doing it.

See those negative words: *don't* and *can't*? Get rid of them. You can do anything if you want it badly enough and can see yourself doing it (or have the vision). Having a positive attitude will get you the kind of success you want.

Use Patience to Produce Results

In class, sometimes you don't "get it" right away. Instead of feeling frustrated, cultivate the habit of patience. Patience is a sign of your personal maturity. You will cope better with your everyday studies if you balance your life and maintain a patient perspective. This does not mean that you should procrastinate. This type of patience is about step-by-step action that leads to results. One class does not add up to a degree, but put several classes on your transcript, and they start to add up. Soon enough, you do get what you set out to achieve: a university degree.

When you are working on your home, sometimes you need a hammer, and other times you need a wrench. Similarly, when you are working toward your degree, sometimes you need to use study tools and other times you need to use stress management or time management tools. Get into the flow as much as possible with your classes and figure out what tools will be the most useful to you. Don't force things to happen. Wait. What you want is a feeling of calm certainty that you are doing the right things in the right way to move toward your degree. This peace of mind allows you to retain more of what you learn and makes you a person whom others enjoy being around.

Procrastination, on the other hand, is just a result of negative thinking. If you tell yourself you *have* to do something, it is the same as if someone else has said that to you. Your subconscious pushes back, and you start thinking of all types of creative ways to get out of doing it.

Instead of becoming frustrated and impatient with a classroom experience, successful students advise others to adopt an attitude and mentality of challenge. Instead of complaining that your instructor doesn't promptly answer your questions or e-mail messages, be grateful for the opportunity to find the answers on your own. The need for answers encourages students to reach out and make friends, as well as learn to work as a team.

If this reasoning seems far-fetched to you, then think of students who are successful. They reach out to others and get the help they need.

They either start a study group or see if they can locate a tutor or an academic coach.

One thing you will find in your classes is a group of people in the same situations you are in. They have daily commitments in addition to being in school that affect their attitudes. Get together and discuss these difficulties. Become one another's support team. Even online, there is often a student chat room in the class for asynchronous student-to-student chat and support. These discussions provide a perfect time to ask other students questions about how they get their assignments done and still maintain sanity. If you make a connection with a class member, perhaps the class itself will become more exciting.

Make Good Impressions

You are making an impression on your instructors with every assignment you turn in. Instructors quickly find out who has a good attitude about the class. And that attitude *does* make a difference in the student's success.

Chronic complainers quickly become the students who are having a difficult time. To be honest, these students don't often get the breaks others do. In fact, we have noticed that other students in the class don't communicate often with the complainers. A poor attitude conveyed through actions hurts only the one with the attitude. Successful students advise others to check their attitudes at the door before they come to class.

One reason that making a good impression is so important is that you may want your professors and/or fellow classmates for references for scholarships and future jobs. Furthermore, those students who decide to go on to graduate school *have* to ask instructors to recommend them. Make sure you have the attitude you need to get the reference or recommendation you want. Instructors usually have many connections and can help you network as you seek your future position. Your positive attitude will go a long way toward ensuring an instructor's or classmate's willingness to stand up for you.

Be Tough

Sometimes you will hear a comment from your instructor or classmates that might offend you. Take the time and have the courage to discuss the perceived offense further; you probably will find that those who made the comments had good intentions.

Part of classroom etiquette and online netiquette is not to be hasty in judgment. Always give people the benefit of the doubt. Assume that all communications are honorable in their intent until absolutely proven otherwise. In other words, don't automatically take every word personally. Some successful students have even commented that it's more than just attitude. "You must have the hide of a rhino," they say.

Be aggressive when it comes to class. Get mentally tough. Your mental toughness will ensure that you get what you want. Keep at it. Remember to revisit that vision of why you are in school—to get that degree. Don't lose that vision. Take all setbacks as temporary, including a bad grade, computer problems, or personal conflicts. When setbacks happen, get in touch with your instructor or school immediately. Let someone know what is going on. That person will often have ideas to assist you through the setback. Do not let setbacks become an excuse to quit.

Focus on Your Strengths

Become committed to you! You deserve the best of everything that you seek. Never sell yourself short. Who signed up for college in the first place? You did. You are the reason you are working so hard. For some, the toughest part of getting a college degree is signing up for the first class. You're already past that part. Your strengths will see you through the rest of the way.

One of the most important strengths all of us have is the ability to be motivated and motivate ourselves. See your motivation as a strength by asking yourself WIIFM (What's In It For Me). When you know your WIIFM, you can use it as a driving force.

You commit to other things in your life the same way. Think about it. You are taking classes because you believe that doing so will help you get where you want to go. Attitudes of success and motivation are developed, not genetic. You can develop a "can-do" attitude.

You can learn any subject. The people who become successful and have astonishing results at meeting their goals are average people who learned and applied the tools to success. If you find that you say, "I can't do it," change it by adding a "yet." I can't do it *yet*. It's "yet" another primary success principle.

Have you heard the saying, "Can't didn't, but try always won"? Those who try are winners because they tried. Those who don't try don't give themselves the opportunity to win. They have already lost.

Challenge the Challenges

Do not let temporary and minor setbacks distract you from your work and goals. You can find creative solutions to these problems. In fact, you are at your creative best when you have a problem to solve.

Another success principle is applicable here: "Success is failure turned inside out" (from the anonymous poem, "Don't Quit"). This is to say that your problems, setbacks, and "failures" can be transformed into successes. How? Learn from your failures and think outside the box for creative solutions to your problems and setbacks.

Do not be disheartened by getting things wrong. When you make a mistake on a quiz or assignment, move on. As Captain James Lawrence said, "Don't give up the ship!" As another saying goes, take college "one day at a time." So what if you have a setback? Pull yourself up, dust yourself off, and smile. Don't think of it as a failure, but as part of the learning process. You are allowed imperfections. They are part of life and can lead to a new growth level for you. Just start over tomorrow. Ask the most successful person you know about this principle, and you will find out what all successful students and people know: Success is built from each mistake or wrong turn.

Be Aware of Scotomas

One way to adjust your attitude is to identify and remove your scotomas. *Scotomas* are blind spots that directly affect your attitude. A typical scotoma that successful students have identified and overcome is one that limits abilities. For example, many students cannot initially appreciate the value of a learner-centered environment until they experience it. Others have a difficult time seeing why it's so important to manage their time and organize their life until they cannot complete an assignment or project on time. The secret key to identifying and removing scotomas is to think outside the box that creates blind spots in your life.

The trouble with being inside a limiting box is that the directions on how to make your life better are outside of the box. This limitation is why you will want to examine your life and study successful people. The tools in this book are one way to get out of your box in terms of what you can do with your academic program.

Another way to get out of your scotoma box is to change your daily routine. For example, pick a different way to drive home from work or school. Open your mind to new possibilities. Highly effective students have an open mind, and they "see" or are willing to see endless possibilities and the truth about themselves. This openness makes them successful.

Dare to Be Great

The difference between mediocrity and greatness is infinitesimally small. For example, the difference between first place and last place in a NASCAR race is often less than four seconds. *Four* seconds! (The difference between first and second place is often less than a tenth of a second!)

The difference between a great baseball hitter and an average hitter is equally small. Those who bat .500 or above—a very small percentage of major league baseball players—are considered great. Mediocre professional baseball players normally bat between .200 and .350. The difference between great and mediocre here is often less than one extra hit every three or four games.

The difference between the winner and loser in the Masters PGA golf championship is normally less than 10 strokes over three days of golf. The difference between first and second place in the Masters is nearly always one stroke over three days of golf.

What makes the difference between mediocrity and greatness? The answer is simple—just a little extra effort. A little extra effort in improving your studying and test-taking skills. A little extra effort in your organizational skills. A little extra effort in developing a great attitude.

Take a moment to view the following online movie on this principle titled *212°: The Extra Degree* (based on the book by Sam Parker and Mac Anderson and available on the Simple Truths website):

www.212movie.com

Conclusion

Attitude is about believing in yourself, knowing that if others (thousands and thousands of others) can get through school, so can you! Be willing to learn from your mistakes. Do not quit. Tell yourself you will do it differently and better next time.

Change your self-talk. Tell yourself that you are going to pass with a good grade. Tell yourself that you do have time. Tell yourself that you can and will do it. Remember what Henry Ford said: "Whether you think you can or you think you can't, you are right." So think you can. Tell yourself that your assignments are challenging, not hard. No matter how much you desire a positive outcome, you will sabotage your efforts if you don't *believe* you can do it. Think positively about the outcome, and realize that you may need to fake a positive attitude until it becomes a habit.

Best Practices: Attitude

Do

- Do develop an attitude of success. Successful students think, plan, and talk success.

- Do persist. "Rest, if you must, but do not quit" (another quote from the anonymous poem "Don't Quit").

- Do challenge yourself and the challenges that face you. Develop an "I can" attitude and implement it always.

- Do focus on ability and possibility. Be self-confident and visualize your dreams.

- Do use the words try, yet, and want to. Empower your subconscious to give you abilities you never knew you had.

- Do recognize your scotomas (blind spots). Open your eyes to new possibilities based on positive attitude adjustments.

- Do be tough. Give others the benefit of the doubt until proven otherwise.

Don't

- Don't succumb to self-doubt. If you don't think you can, you probably can't.

- Don't give up. Learn to roll with the punches and get up, dust yourself off, and move ahead.

- Don't settle for mediocrity. Don't sell yourself short of excellence. Go the extra few inches to become great.

Assignment 5.1: Identify Your Blind Spots

In this assignment, you identify five things you don't think you can do, and then identify the blind spots that prevent you from seeing the solutions. By doing this, you offer yourself a "can-do" attitude and literally ensure your success as a student.

1. Write down the five things you don't think you can do.

   _____

   _____

   _____

   _____

   _____

2. Identify the blind spots preventing you from accomplishing your five goals.

   _____

   _____

   _____

   _____

   _____

3. Save this list to share with your class.

CHAPTER 6

Goal Setting

"To reach your goals and dreams, it is essential to learn the specifics of goal setting that get results."

Dr. Karine Blackett, author of *Career Achievement: Growing Your Goals*

Highly effective students must be goal oriented. You need to be able to see the light at the end of the tunnel, and, no, it is not a train coming at you. Remaining goal oriented can be difficult if you are a student who is plugging away at your degree, all the while juggling many responsibilities. If you are a nontraditional student, you probably have a job you are contending with, classes, and family. You are expected to be in 20 places at once.

The same applies to traditional students. You might have classes, as well as a family of your own or family stresses far away. You might be in collegiate sports programs or in a study-intensive program. You might even have to take a part-time or full-time job to meet your financial needs. You also need to find a way to see the end, to keep in mind the success principle that states, "You will move toward what you think about the most."

If you maintain a positive attitude but don't have a goal in mind, your diploma will remain an elusive dream.

Set SMART Goals

Successful students always set goals. One suggestion for setting goals is to write your goals on your calendar or put them in your electronic calendar. Before you do, make sure your goals are SMART. SMART stands for

Specific

Measurable

Attainable

Realistic

Tangible

Is your goal specific? A vague goal, such as "Get better grades," does not fill the bill for a good goal. A specific goal, such "Get an A in Accounting 102," does fill the bill.

Is your goal measurable? Something that is not measurable is generally not attainable. The preceding example of the goal to "Get an A in Accounting 102" is measurable in that it states an "A" letter grade.

Is your goal attainable? Is it really something you can have or just a pipe dream? For example, an unattainable goal for most of us would be "Become the King of England after completing my degree." Something more attainable might be "Become a vice president of XYZ Technology company after completing my MBA degree."

Is your goal realistic? Although it is closely related to the standard of setting an attainable goal, this check forces us to look a little deeper. In the preceding example, if one of the requirements of becoming a vice president for XYZ Technology is four years of on-the-job experience and you have only six months of experience, the goal is probably not realistic unless you qualify it to include "…gain three more years of experience and…" It is good to have high expectations of yourself, but just keep them real. It can go the other way also. If you get a four-year degree, raise your expectations. Know that you are going to get a better job than working for minimum wage at the local drive-through, fast-food restaurant.

Is your goal tangible? Is it something you can touch, feel, see, taste, or smell? A degree is tangible. When you have that diploma in your hand and the job offer of your dreams, you will understand just how tangible it is.

See the End

Making goals is easier if you look at the end first. What do you want to do when you graduate? What kind of degree do you want? What kind of lifestyle do you want? The dreams that you are visualizing will help you set goals. Keep your "eye on the prize." Remind yourself often of the larger picture, and focus on that positive outcome, whether it be a better job, new home, more money, or being a positive role model for your children. Just remember what your goals are.

As you establish long-range goals, you should also set short-range ones. Decide what you want to get out of each course you take and how it can improve you. Think of how what you are learning will apply to your career. It may help for you to post a list of your goals in the area where you are studying. Include the grade you are working toward, or the degree you are seeking. Seeing the "prize" in writing near your place of study or in a place you frequently look (such as on the mirror) will help you concentrate on both the long-term and short-term goals.

Check Your Attitude

After you set your goals, make sure your attitude takes you closer to your goals. Keeping a positive attitude means believing in yourself and working toward your goals.

Does having a positive attitude mean you have to be cheerful all the time? No. Your overall attitude is more important than your day-to-day mood. You can be serious, happy, or whatever mood you choose. If you plant watermelon seeds and work the field, it does not matter whether you are in a certain mood; you will get watermelons. As long as you keep working toward your goals, you will eventually achieve them.

That being said, you may have a more enjoyable process if you and others like your moods. That is a choice.

Everyone feels frustrated, overwhelmed, or angry from time to time. When you focus on a problem or beat yourself up with your own negative self-talk, immediately replace it with a constructive thought. If you need a session to complain, give yourself one, but time it (less than 15 minutes) and warn people around you that you are taking one. Then go for it. Let your frustration out. Like a storm clears the air, such venting sessions can clear your mind so that you can get back to the task at hand. Laugh at yourself after your complaining session.

Remember that stumbling blocks are just stepping stones in disguise, and a problem can be an opportunity. Keep your goals and desires in the back and front of your mind and keep working. It has been said that persistence is the blood brother to success. Do something—anything— to move forward to your goal. Rest if needed, but keep at it.

Have Faith

We have all heard the cliché, "You gotta have faith." And successful students have identified faith as an important ingredient for setting goals. Faith is by definition "the substance of things hoped for and the evidence of things not seen (Hebrews 11:1)." In terms of goals, faith is the confidence and trust you have that you can and will be more than you currently are.

An analogy for understanding faith follows the story of a young driver who has completed driver's education, the driver's examination, and three months of driving experience on the open road and in the city streets. This young person is confident in his abilities. He trusts his judgment, and others trust his skills. However, when the snow falls and the streets become icy, he has to have faith (confident trust) that he can use what he knows to make it from point A to point B, because he has never faced these conditions before.

The road to your diploma may become slippery, but you gotta have faith that you can achieve your degree, job, and lifestyle goals in any conditions. So what if you put it in the ditch a time or two? As long as you are willing to learn from your mistakes and press on, you will succeed. Have faith! Know and believe that you can reach your destination even though you are not there yet.

Recognize That a Goal Without Work Is a Wish

When you sit down to think of your goals, make them realistic enough to see them, yet far enough out to give you the creative drive to get them. You want to do both: Set clear, realistic, and attainable goals, as well as set large goals that you can reach by chunking them into smaller goals, like stepping stones. If you set goals too close to what you know you can attain, then your life will remain the same. Tomorrow will look a lot like yesterday.

Build on the success principle that states, "You will move toward and become like that which you think about the most *and with the strongest emotions.*" When you know what you want, visualize it, and know it is yours. Picture yourself having or accomplishing that goal. What you focus on will expand, so focus on goals and the life you seek. Remember, the life you seek is also seeking you.

To get the drive to go where you want to go, set some "in a perfect life" goals. What would you have, do, or be if you were living your perfect life? Suspend your critical mind and write down some goals that you have a passion for. Forget about the "how." Just write them down.

You can expand this goal-setting exercise beyond your academic goals, as your career and academic goals will support each other. In other words, if you have a goal of having a certain income, then getting your degree might be a step in that direction. Chunking the long-term goal of getting your diploma into several short-term, stepping-stone goals for your classes will help you move toward your diploma goal and ultimately your income goal.

Assignment 6.1: Identify the Negatives

Before you can proceed in the direction of your dreams, you must identify the negatives that hold you back. In this assignment, you not only identify the negatives, you also turn them inside out until they are positives.

(continued)

(continued)

1. Write down all the things that are negatives in your life right now. What are the things that wear you down, scare you, and/or make you sad?

   _____

   _____

   _____

   _____

   _____

   _____

2. Reverse each item as though you were reversing a negative of a picture. What is the opposite? If you wrote down that you don't have enough money to pay your bills, write down that you have more than enough money to pay your bills easily. Keep writing until you have reversed all of your negative statements.

   _____

   _____

   _____

   _____

   _____

   _____

3. Transform all the positive statements into specific goals. Envision a true story for your life.

   _____

   _____

   _____

   _____

   _____

   _____

4. Date this worksheet, make a copy of it, and put it someplace where you can look at it often.

Assignment 6.2: Recognize the Consequences

Based on the assumption that you have a goal of graduating, this assignment helps you focus on why graduating is more important than quitting. The result should enable you to work more effectively and efficiently toward your goal.

1. Get two pieces of paper, and then draw a horizontal line in the middle of each paper, dividing it in half.

2. On each piece of paper, draw a vertical line that divides the upper half into two sections. You should end up with two quarters in the top half and one full half in the lower half of each paper.

3. Write conflicting goals at the top of each paper. For example, you could put "Earn My Degree" on one paper and "Work More" on the other.

4. For each goal, list its advantages or the reasons you could choose it in the upper-left quarter of the paper. (If you get stuck, you might ask others to help you with your list.)

5. In the upper-right quarter, write or list the inconveniences, disadvantages, or reasons that the goal is not a good option.

6. After you list the positives and negatives for each goal, write "The Future" in the bottom section of each paper.

7. Using the lists of positives and negatives, write the results of following any of the lines of thinking.

When you see these results written in black and white, you can foresee the results of each goal. You are then able to set goals that are based on the choices you need to make to have the future you desire.

The purpose of these exercises is to get you beyond inertia. They can put motivation behind your goals. After you plot this out, it is no longer a dream. It is not based on your imagination. It is your future reality.

Always ask yourself if what you are about to do takes you away from your goals or closer to them. If it is further away, just say "no."

Plan for Setbacks

Having obstacles in your path is not a bad thing. In fact, it has been said that hitting roadblocks and feeling frustrated is a sign that you chose worthy goals because you want them! If you can predict roadblocks, all the better; you can anticipate in advance how you might get through them. Think about what might go wrong and how you would deal with it. What will you do, for example, if your computer crashes? You can ask friends if you can use their computers. You can also find a computer lab in the library you can use. Now you are ready to let that potential roadblock go to the side. Remember that what you focus on expands, and worrying is actually negative goal setting.

If you are expecting everything to go smoothly all the time, you are going to be disappointed. Rather, see the problems as opportunities to reach your goals. Remember the poem line that "Success is failure turned inside out," so do not be dismayed by setbacks.

Stay Focused in Online Classes

Most students who take classes on the Internet do so because they lack time to attend classes in a traditional setting. If you are an online student, remember that you must succeed as a self-directed learner. You may not have the same prodding that on-campus students have. Your professor and friends won't be in your face, reminding you when you need to be in class, when assignments are due, and where you should be in your reading. You have to keep track of it all and make sure it gets done. Successful online students always set goals.

You know how to organize, you have tools for studying and test taking, you know your learning style and personality type, and you have a positive attitude. Now take it one step further and set goals. Set goals as to when you are going to finish assignments and where you should be in your studying by specific dates on your calendar. You may find it difficult at the beginning of that first semester or quarter to remember when things need to be done. Always keep in mind that, as an online student especially, you are responsible for your success. Review the goal-setting tools in this chapter, and you can have your cake and eat it, too!

Reward Yourself

When you achieve a goal, remember to give yourself a reward—no matter how small. Have fun and learn to celebrate your successes! Make sure that you tell yourself how proud you are that you received a good grade on your paper or test. Give yourself some treat, such as an ice cream cone for a small achievement or a larger treat for a greater achievement: Get a new outfit, go to a movie, or whatever you choose. Just make sure you do something so that your subconscious will continue to strive to achieve the rewards.

Conclusion

Visualize the long- and short-term picture of your success. With each class, remember the end goal and keep visualizing yourself attaining it. If your goal is getting a degree, graduating with honors, or attaining financial independence, see yourself already there. Consider taking a picture of yourself in a cap and gown. When you see the end result, you can keep going even (or rather, especially) when you face obstacles.

Best Practices: Goal Setting

Do

- Do see the end. Find out where you want to go, and you will get there as you set goals.

- Do write SMART goals. Vague and unspecific goals will result in a vague and unspecific experience.

- Do think both long and short term. There are important victories to be had in meeting short-term goals that can propel you toward the long-term ones.

- Do check your attitude. You can have the occasional bad mood, but continue to plow the field.

(continued)

(continued)

- Do have faith in yourself. Be confident in your abilities and trust that you will succeed.

- Do recognize failure as an opportunity to succeed, as long as you self-correct as you go. Success is always failure turned inside out.

- Do reward yourself. Celebrate achievements. Celebrating is more important than most people think.

Don't

- Don't think you can't. If you think you can't, then you won't. It's as simple and as difficult as that.

- Don't begin without seeing the end. Short-term goals without long-term dreams, vision, and goals will shortchange you.

- Don't expect to achieve your goals without work. Without work, goals are just dreams.

Assignment 6.3: Search the Web for Goal Setting

1. Using the search engine of your choice, locate a website that deals with goal setting. You can use the following links or find your own with a keyword search on goal setting:

   www.mindtools.com/page6.html

   www.projectsmart.co.uk/smart-goals.html

2. Find three helpful tips you would use in goal setting.

3. Write down the URL of the website and the three tips to share with your class:

   _____

   _____

   _____

CHAPTER 7

Basic Research Skills

"By seeking and blundering we learn."

Johann Wolfgang von Goethe

At the university level, you will have to write research papers and complete projects during your academic career. You need to be able to find information from a variety of sources, sort through and organize that information, form opinions about it, and write research papers at the university and college level without *plagiarizing* (using someone else's information, passing it off as your own, and not giving credit to the source where you found that information). When you learn how to do research, writing research papers becomes second nature.

Reading this chapter isn't going to make you a research genius, but it will guide you and give you information that will help you do a better job in deciding how to find reliable, valid information. You won't feel so "dazed and confused" by all the sources of information available to you. This chapter will make you a better problem solver because it gives you the tools to do a better job of evaluating information.

Become Information Literate

As you go through your academic career, you will be asked this question more and more frequently: "Are you information literate?" But what does the term *information literate* mean?

The American Library Association defines *information literacy* as "the set of abilities requiring individuals to recognize when information is needed and [to] have the ability to locate, evaluate, and use effectively the needed information." Becoming information literate means not only that you can find information, but also that you can use critical thinking skills. Critical thinking, put simply, is problem solving.

You will realize how important it is to become information literate in all aspects of your life. Many people, including educators, are not information literate. Get a step ahead and make sure that you are. Be able to find the information you need.

We live in a society in which people want information, but they want it now, and they want someone else to get it for them. Don't fall into the trap of "fast is better." Don't expect anyone to hold your hand and guide you to the information you need. Take the responsibility for conducting your own research. This doesn't mean that you can't get help. You just can't learn how to find information if you aren't willing to do the work. When you get the hang of finding information and are comfortable with using a variety of sources of information, you will be surprised how much knowledge you will gain. You will increase your academic potential by leaps and bounds.

For more information on information literacy, you can go to this website:

www.ala.org/ala/mgrps/divs/acrl/issues/infolit

Know How to Locate Reliable, Valid Information

In starting the research process, you need to be able to locate reliable, valid information. You should become familiar with knowing where to find and evaluate books and periodicals in hard copy as well as those subscribed to in electronic format. You also need to be able to evaluate other resources found on the World Wide Web and know that most of these resources should be used with caution.

What is reliable, valid information? Where do you find it? We as a society are engulfed in information these days. The problem we encounter is determining how to wade through this deluge of information to find what we need.

Students always come to us totally mystified and confused as to what information they should use. Their instructor has told them, "You can't use the Internet for your resources." Their librarian has told them to make sure they use the electronic resources (e-resources) found online. The students say, "But my professor told me I cannot use the Internet for resources. Aren't the e-resources on the Internet?" These conflicting instructions can be very confusing. Let's sort it all out.

The Three General Categories of Resources

Think of research resources as tools you will use to find information. We have divided the resources into three general categories: traditional, reserves, and electronic.

Traditional Resources

Traditional resources are those items found, for the most part, in the library setting. They include paper (hard copy) versions of books, journals, magazines, newspapers, and publications. Other traditional resources are microfiche, videos, slides, CDs, and any other media types.

The nontraditional student, who is not as computer literate or savvy as others who have used computers since grade school, prefers to use traditional resources. This reluctance to use e-resources is disappearing quickly. Once most nontraditional students find out how easy and convenient e-resources are to use, they prefer them to traditional resources. Using traditional resources is fine, as there will always be the need for them. To be information literate, however, you must to learn to use the variety of resources available to you.

Reserves

Reserves are handouts, notes, books, and other items that the professor asks to be available for students to use in a special location. These items have a shorter loan period. Students can check them out for one hour, three hours, or as long as overnight. Sometimes the items are put in *closed reserves,* which means they can't be checked out and can be used only on the premises. The professor uses this type of reserve in order to make sure that all the students in the class have access to the resources.

E-resources

E-resources (electronic resources) are information you access and use on a computer. You can find an abundance of information in electronic format *online,* which means via the Internet. In fact, most universities offer classes via the Internet now. If you are a student who attends classes on campus or online, you most likely will be doing *most* of your research online.

Many students prefer using virtual (online) resources so that they don't have to lug heavy books around. Another reason students are using e-resources is that most of these resources are available 24/7. With an Internet connection or wifi, you can look for information on your computer at home, on your laptop, or have it downloaded to your cell phone day or night. The electronic format makes searching for information very easy. The important issue, though, is to make certain that you are using the correct e-resources and getting reliable, valid information.

Campus Information Sources

Universities and colleges offer several options on how to get information on the research resources available to you. Following are a few places where you probably can find this information:

- **The information packet mailed to you when you were accepted into college.** Make sure you read through any mailings you receive from your school. Information on what resources are available along with your login and passwords for those resources are usually found in this information.

- **The new-student orientation, usually held a few weeks before classes start.** The orientation can be anywhere from one day in length to a week and can include pretesting for class placement, along with student advisor information, class schedules, and information about available resources. Make the effort to attend orientation.

- **Freshman success classes.** Freshman are usually required to take these classes offered by the school, where they learn study skills, time management, test-taking skills, money management, and the resources available for research.

- **Library research class.** Because of the overwhelming amount of information and the increase in types of formats in which you can find information, most schools now offer a semester- or term-long library research class. We consider this class one of the most valuable and urge you to take it. Not only will you learn about the resources available to you, you also will learn how to use them.

- **The library.** Find out where the library is located. Most libraries have handouts and online tutorials about the resources they offer and how to use them.

Begin Your Research with Books

To research a topic for a paper, begin by looking for appropriate books. Most research papers require you to find some of your information from books whether they be e-books or hard copy books. Books give a more in-depth and varied coverage of a subject than do other resources, such as magazine or journal articles.

The books you choose should

- **Contain information that is relevant to your topic.**

- **Be current.** Check publication dates. Make sure the material in the book is not dated (old). When you are looking for information about current government policy, for example, you don't want to grab the first book you find on government policy and call it good—especially if it was written in 1998. If you are comparing government policy of the 1990s with the policy now, then you can use older materials as well.

Hard Copy Books

You can find hard copy books in a library by searching its online catalog, discussed later in this chapter. Make sure that you know how to search for books by author, title, subject, and keyword. A staff person in your library can show you how to use the online catalog, or the library will have tutorials available for you. If you are not sure how to navigate the online catalog, make the independent learner in you take over. Click the Help menu. Then take the time to read some hints on how to conduct a search. If you still are having problems, ask for assistance. The library staff is there to help you.

Electronic Books

More books are becoming available in an electronic format. These books are usually found in the electronic resources available at your library. Additionally, the "information deluge" has brought with it several e-book vendors with their databases.

Some common names you will see associated with e-books are

- NetLibrary
- Jones e-global
- Questia
- LearningExpress

The most important thing for you to do is to find out from your librarian which e-book database(s) your school has available for you. Associate the name of each database with e-books. You also can buy e-books from book vendors online such as Amazon (www.amazon.com) and Barnes & Noble (www.barnesandnoble.com). Amazon has the Kindle, an electronic reading device that you can get with wifi that is very affordable. The e-books to download are usually less expensive than regular hard copy books.

The great thing about e-books is you don't have to lug a book around with you. With the new electronic reading devices you can easily relax and read as the devices are not cumbersome or heavy. Using e-books allows you to read the book on your computer screen or electronic reading device. You don't have to worry about losing the book or not getting it back on the date it is due.

Vendors such as NetLibrary have tools available for you to use while you are reading the book. Most will have a dictionary in the database so you can look up definitions of words you do not understand. NetLibrary has a useful Note feature that you can click on in order to take notes as you read. If you use the Note feature, you can keep track of where you are in the book if your reading gets interrupted. When you come back to the book, you can remember where you were by looking at your notes.

Regardless of the e-book source your school uses, you should know what the source is, how to access it, how to find a book, and how to read that book online. You should also be able to use the tools that e-book sources have available. Once again, check with a member of the library staff to discover the type(s) of e-books available for you to use and how to access that information. The school library should have tutorials or "how-to" information in hard copy and online that give you step-by-step instructions on accessing and using e-books. You should be able to search for e-books from your online library catalog.

Become Comfortable with Using Periodicals in Your Research

Periodicals are publications that come in sequence or order, including journals, magazines, and newspapers. Differences among periodicals can be determined using the following criteria:

- Type of publisher

- Audience

- Qualifications of author or authors

- Level of coverage

- Bibliography or references

- Format

- Advertising

- Index

The following sections discuss the differences between the three main types of periodicals used for research and their characteristics: scholarly or research journals, magazines, and professional or trade journals.

You will hear professors say you must get your information from a juried publication or a peer-reviewed publication or a publication that is not only juried or peer-reviewed but also is found in the electronic database that the school subscribes to. Don't panic. It isn't that difficult. The sections that follow also discuss what is meant by *peer-reviewed* and *juried*.

Scholarly or Research Journals

Many publications have the word *journal* in their titles, but that doesn't mean they are true journals. They are true journals only if they include scholarly research. Scholarly or research journals have these characteristics:

- May be *juried* or refereed; that is, an editorial board of experts (the authors' peers, hence the term *peer-reviewed*) examines the articles before publication to ensure the quality of the article.

- Are published to foster ideas and present new ideas.

- Are usually published by institutions of higher education.

- List authors' affiliations and credentials.

- Target other researchers or scholars in the field as their audience.

- Contain articles of primary research (research done by the authors themselves) and include a methods section describing how the authors went about conducting the research.

- Include extensive bibliographies or reference lists of articles.

- Contain little or no advertising.

- Are often arranged as paginated volumes. (For example, if one issue ends on page 230, the next issue will start on page 231.)

- Have an *abstract* (brief summary) for each article to help the reader evaluate the article and decide whether it is worth using in the research process.

- Often have narrow focus on a specific subject area.

- Are indexed in subject-specific indexes or databases.

Magazines

Magazines, published for interest-specific audiences, may or may not have quality material. They are not taken as seriously as scholarly journals. Their main purpose is to generate subscription and advertising sales. Magazines have these characteristics:

- Are published by a commercial publisher.

- Target audiences by demographics—age, gender, interest, and so on.

- Usually do not provide authors' credentials.

- Never contain primary research, so no methods section is included.

- Do not provide bibliography or reference lists.

- Do not include bibliographies or reference lists of articles.

- Contain colorful, attention-getting ads.

- Do not provide abstracts of articles.

- May be indexed.

Professional or Trade Journals

Trade journals are "do it yourself manuals" for professionals and practitioners in a certain field. These periodicals can resemble both scholarly journals and magazines and share the following characteristics:

- Are published by professional or trade organizations, such as the American Library Association.

- Target an audience of other professionals or practitioners.

- Usually give authors' affiliations and credentials.

- Have limited advertising, directed to a specific trade or profession.

- Offer very limited or no bibliographies.

- Sometimes contain primary research *(Journal of American Medical Association)* or secondary research *(American Libraries)*.

- Are not peer-reviewed or juried.

- Are indexed in subject and general indexes or databases.

Hard Copy Periodicals

Schools and universities usually have several hard copy journals, magazines, and newspapers available. If you are searching for peer-reviewed journals in hard copy in the library, pay attention to the criteria listed earlier. This is where those critical thinking skills come in. Take the list with you and try to find peer-reviewed journals on your own.

To find articles in hard copy periodicals, you will need to find an index. An *index* is a separate book, journal supplement, CD, or listing that provides accurate references to articles in a number of different periodicals. The index in the library can be in hard copy, on CD, or online.

Many periodicals have indexes with unique features, but these indexes also have some characteristics in common. You can search indexes by authors or by subject. Some indexes include abstracts of the contents of each article. Ask a library staff person what indexes are available and where you can find them.

After you locate the indexes, you can look for the articles. If you need information on gun control, for example, you can look up gun control in the index. Under the words *gun control* is a list of the articles that contain information on gun control. The list gives the article title, author, journal

Note: Do not highlight the information unless you photocopy the article. Librarians do not appreciate you highlighting the magazines and journals.

or magazine containing the article, and the date of its publication. When you have a list of articles you want to read, take that list, go to the periodicals section of the library, and locate the journals or magazines you need. When you have found the articles, photocopy them, read through them in the library or at home, and highlight the information you plan on using in your paper.

Electronic Resources

Terms such as *Internet resources* and *electronic subscription resources* can confuse students. The confusion arises from the fact that most universities and schools now have journal, magazine, and newspaper articles available in full text from electronic subscription resources, or electronic databases as some are called, that are online. Some of the most well-known electronic resources are ProQuest, EBSCO and NetLibrary, FirstSearch, and Jones e-global library, to name just a few.

If the *New England Journal of Medicine* is available from ProQuest, for example, you can search for a journal article in that database. You can choose which articles you want and then either read them online or print them out to read later. The school subscribes to these resources by paying a fee for the use of the service. (This is where some of your tuition money is going.)

Because not everyone has access to these resources, you will hear them referred to as "the invisible Web." You can use the Internet to get to the website of ProQuest, for example, but you can't use its resources without a login and password or you have to gain access through your online library page. These resources are part of the Internet, but they are not available to everyone. So when a professor tells you not to use the Internet for research, he is not referring to these type of resources. He just doesn't want you to go to Google or Yahoo! and use a keyword search for information. He is telling you to use the reliable resources, both online and on campus, that your library has available for you to use instead.

Accessing Electronic Resources

The logins and passwords for electronic resources are usually found in orientation materials you were given in a freshman orientation class or in materials that were sent to you when you became a student. Many universities have the resources available to you on one Web page accessed through a proxy server where you will need to use a login and password only one time to access most of the information. If you didn't get that information, contact your school library and ask for information about the services available for library research. The staff member will get you in touch with the right person.

If you are on campus, you will usually find that libraries offer some type of class on library research or offer seminars or workshops on using the resources. A member of the library staff usually visits a freshman orientation class to give students information on available resources. You can ask a staff member for help or use the services of the academic coaches or tutors.

To complicate matters a bit, most electronic resources have several databases available, depending on what your school has subscribed to. When schools subscribe to electronic databases, they can choose different types of packages. For example, if you are attending a school that has ProQuest and offers degrees in business, the school probably offers ABI/INFORM, a database containing business journals and magazines. If you are getting a nursing degree, your school will provide databases where you will be able to find medical information. An example would be CINAHL from EBSCO, which is a database that allows students to search for articles and information in the nursing field. Schools usually purchase databases that provide information for all their academic programs.

You will want to become familiar with such databases. If you aren't sure, use those critical thinking skills and either ask for help or click on the database listing to see all the databases available from that service and what is contained in that database. Don't be afraid to click on buttons and find information.

Whether you are conducting your research at home or in the library, remember that most electronic subscription databases have a Help menu. The Help menu will give you some pointers on basic searching and other useful ways to find the information you need.

Most university libraries have a link to all the electronic databases on their library Web page. They more than likely will also have an E-mail Your Librarian link on the Web page. When in doubt, ask someone for help. Get in touch with a library staff person at your school and find out how to access electronic resources. Then learn how to use them.

Searching for Information in Electronic Resources

When you are trying to find magazine articles in an electronic subscription resource, you will want to become familiar with the databases in that resource. So if you are a nursing student, for example, select the medical database that contains the information you need, rather than searching all the databases available.

The great thing about most electronic resources is that you can limit your search. By either clicking on a check box found on your search page or by clicking on Advanced Search, you should be able to search for only peer-reviewed or juried articles, for articles by date (articles published after 2008 only, for example), or for journals in specific publications. Limiting your search in those areas will make your search for information much easier.

Following are some basic search tips that work in most electronic databases. Again, if you don't understand how to do a search, seek help in your library. If all else fails, find the word *Help* and click on it. It will tell you what you need to do to find information.

- **Use quotation marks (" ") to search for exact phases.**

- **Use more than one word in your searches.** If you are looking for an article about poisonous snakes, for example, don't just search for *snakes*. First, you will get way too many *hits* (results). Second, you then would have to read through the hits, hoping to find the word *poisonous*. Search for "poisonous snakes" instead. If you are looking for poisonous snakes from Brazil, try searching for "poisonous snakes in Brazil."

- **Use a *Boolean* search.** This type of search contains *operators* (words that broaden or narrow your search) such as the following:

  - **AND.** When you use the word *AND* in a search, the database finds *all* the words. In a search entered as "economics and war," for example, the database looks for an article containing both those words.

- **AND NOT.** When you use the words *AND NOT*, the database finds articles that have the first word, but not the second word. A search entered as "Internet and not HTML," for example, finds just "Internet."

- **OR.** When you use the word *OR*, the database finds articles with any of the words. A search entered as "Internet OR intranet," for example, finds articles containing either of the two terms.

Although many other types of Boolean searches are available, those listed are the most commonly used. For other advanced searching tips, use the Help menu within the specific database.

Use Interlibrary Loans

Sometimes you might find a book in a reading list or hear about a book that you know will be helpful in your research, and then find that it isn't available at your university or school library or the nearest public library. Ask a library staff member at your school whether an interlibrary loan service is available. Many universities have that service available for students as a free service; others may charge a small fee.

The same is true of articles. While you are searching for a journal article, you might see that it is available only as an abstract or summary. Again, get the bibliographic information (title of journal, article title, and date of publication). Interlibray loans today are usually submitted through your online library Web page. Universities use services such as ILLiad, WorldCat Resource Sharing, or some other popular service. Make sure you fill out the form with all important information to assure that you get the correct book or article through the service.

Approach the World Wide Web with Caution

We are not going to explain the entire Internet concept to you. The important thing to know is that the Internet is a way of connecting computers to each other so that they can exchange information, and the World Wide Web is just part of the Internet. (Before the development of the World Wide Web, computers exchanged information via Telnet, which transferred only text files.) The World Wide Web is the part of the Internet with all the pretty little Web pages and pictures and text that you find at Web addresses.

Regarding research and the Internet, we want you to understand the differences in the reliability of the information available on a typical website and the electronic resources you can access through your school's online library portal. Even some instructors get confused when they say you can't use Internet resources or Web resources. What they actually mean is that you need to use the resources provided to you by your university or college library. Your instructors don't want you to just base your research on websites because that information may not be valid or reliable. And you want your information to be as unbiased and reliable as possible.

Keep in mind that anyone can have a Web page. Iona Information can put anything she wants on a Web page. Does that make the information correct, reliable, or valid? Not necessarily. If Iona is pro-gun control, for example, she can create a Web page and post inaccurate statistics on it. She can claim that 1,000 people died last year from gunshot wounds in Rapid City, South Dakota, when only 3 people died from gunshot wounds. If students use that inaccurate statistic in their papers, their papers are inaccurate.

The most important statement about researching that we can make is that the resources you should use most of the time are those available to you through your university or public library—the subscription electronic resources. Only as a last resort should you use Web resources that are not subscription resources.

Does that mean that none of the information on the Web is reliable and valid? No. The top-level *domain* part of a website's address can tell you a lot about the legitimacy of the site. Sites ending in

- .edu are links to college-based Web pages.
- .org are nonprofit organizations.
- .gov indicate governmental departments or agencies.
- .mil are U.S. military organizations and are reliable for statistical information.
- .com are commercial sites, online services, or for-profit businesses.
- .net are networking and business organizations.

Some sites, especially those in the .gov, .net, .edu, and .mil domains (and even some .com sites), have some reliable, valid information.

Let's say you have found most of your information in books, e-books, journals, and magazines, in both hard copy and in electronic format. You also may have found a website with some information that wasn't in your other sources, but you want to use it for your paper. Should you? To answer this question, use the following guidelines and questions to determine whether the information on a particular website is valid and reliable. The more questions you can answer with a "yes," the more reliable the website is likely to be.

- **Is the information accurate, reliable, and error-free?** To find out, determine the answers to the following questions:
  - Can the information be verified?
  - Are sources listed?
  - Is the author clearly identified?
  - Are the author's qualifications or background listed?
  - Do the author's qualifications indicate that he or she is an expert on the topic?
  - Is the publisher or organization presenting the information reputable?

  Web standards to ensure accuracy are still being developed, so being aware of the possibility of inaccuracy is very important.

- **Is the information objective?** Ask these questions:
  - Is the information presented with a minimum of bias?
  - Does the material focus on presenting information to the audience instead of persuading the audience?
  - Does the information focus on facts instead of personal opinion?

  The goals of those presenting the information are often not clearly stated.

- **Is the information current?** Ask these questions:
  - Are dates provided that indicate when the information was written, posted, and updated?
  - Is the information up to date?

  The publication date should be clearly labeled.

- **Is the coverage thorough?** Ask these questions:
  - Can you easily identify what topics the site addresses?
  - Are the topics explored in detail or depth?
  - Is the Web coverage similar to the coverage in print resources?
  - Is the extent of the Web coverage easy to determine?

- **Is the website itself reliable?** Ask these questions:
  - Has the site had an enduring presence on the Web?
  - Are unknown parties blocked from altering the site? That is, is it clear who has provided the content on the site?

Conclusion

Just reading through this chapter puts you well on your way to becoming information literate. Do you know all the answers? Certainly not, but you will be more comfortable as you use the library and its resources to research topics. You will be able to find the information you need from a variety of resources, evaluate that information, and use it in the correct way. Keep your site addresses for your e-resources handy. Get in the habit of using them instead of those in the .com domain. If you feel lost or don't understand something, remember to ask for help.

For more information, search on the following headings on YouTube (www.youtube.com). Check out the videos. They will be great help to you in using electronic resources and understanding how to use your college library.

In the search box, type in the following:

College library help

Electronic resources

Evaluating library resources

Evaluating websites

Best Practices: Library Research

Do

- Do become information literate.

- Do know what is good information and where to find it.

- Do find out what resources your school library has available.

- Do know how to access electronic subscription database resources.

- Do ask for help and see your school librarian or an academic coach.

- Do know what style or format should be used in writing your paper.

- Do know how to cite resources correctly—find out what style you should be using (see Chapter 8, "Research Paper Writing" for more information about this).

Don't

- Don't procrastinate getting started on your research.

- Don't get discouraged when looking for information—ask for help.

- Don't use a nonsubscription website unless you can't find the information you need anywhere else and you are sure that the website is accurate, reputable, unbiased, current, and thorough.

Assignment 7.1: Conduct a Library Search

If you are an on-campus student, find the answers to all the following questions. If you are an online student, answer only questions 11 through 16.

If the librarian was unable to visit your class, then you have to use those wonderful critical thinking skills and find the answers to these questions on your own. Go to your school library and find a staff

(continued)

(continued)

member who can answer the questions. Get a classmate to help you find the answers. Learn how to use the resources together.

If you are an online student and do not have a campus near you, find out the address to the library Web page and find out the answers through viewing the Web page. If you can't find some of the answers, e-mail the campus librarian.

1. Where is your university or college library located?

_____

_____

_____

2. What is the Web address for the college library Web page?

_____

3. What information can be found on the library Web page?

_____

_____

_____

4. When is the library open?

_____

_____

_____

5. Where are the journals and magazines kept?

_____

_____

_____

6. Does the library have a list of journals and magazines? Where is the list?

_____

_____

_____

7. Can you take reference materials out of the library?

_____

8. Can you take magazines out of the library?

_____

9. What is the borrowing period for books?

_____

_____

10. How many books can you check out at one time?

_____

_____

11. What is the Web address of the online catalog in which you can search for books?

_____

_____

_____

12. What electronic subscription database resources are available for you to use?

_____

_____

_____

(continued)

(continued)

13. Where can you find the Web addresses for those resources?

_____

_____

14. Where can you find the logins and passwords for those resources?

_____

_____

_____

15. Does your school library have tutorials or student guides on how to use those resources? If so, where can you find them?

_____

_____

_____

16. Does your library have an interlibrary loan service? If yes, what is the name of the service and how do you access it?

_____

_____

When you have the questions and answers put down on paper, you will have the information available to you when you get ready to do your research. You may think that 16 questions is a lot of questions to answer. But not only do you need to find the answers to these questions, you need to learn how to use the resources they point to as well. Motivate yourself: Tell yourself you want to learn these things because you will not only be a better student, you also will be successful at doing your research.

Assignment 7.2: Search the Web for Library Skills

Go to the website that lists information literacy standards for student learning:

     www.ala.org/aasl/standards

Read through the descriptions for each standard. Then answer these questions:

1. Do you consider yourself to be information literate? Why or why not?

_____

_____

_____

_____

_____

_____

2. What does standard 1 mean to you? (Explain your answer in a paragraph.)

_____

_____

_____

_____

_____

_____

_____

(continued)

(continued)

3. What does standard 2 mean to you? (Explain your answer in a paragraph.)

_____

_____

_____

_____

_____

_____

4. What does standard 3 mean to you? (Explain your answer in a paragraph.)

_____

_____

_____

_____

_____

_____

5. What does standard 4 mean to you? (Explain your answer in a paragraph.)

_____

_____

_____

_____

_____

_____

CHAPTER 8

Research Paper Writing

"Whatever you attempt, go at it with spirit.
Do what is expected—and then some."

Anonymous

Many college students have been out of the academic setting for a long time. You may be one of those who have forgotten some of the basics of writing a research paper. In this chapter, we give you a basic outline to help jog your memory and get you started down the right path to the correct way to write a research paper. This chapter also presents some of the most important aspects about the process of writing a research paper and some dangers to avoid.

The Academic Writing Process

Before you can turn your paper in, you must complete several tasks. Many times you will see students writing papers in a computer lab, and you might be rather surprised at the writing techniques they use. Many write as they read the information for their papers. You might also see many students writing with no information; they find their resources to cite after they have written their papers.

Here is a little-known secret: Professors actually read your papers, and they know when you don't use the resources you are citing. As you will read in later sections, they also can tell whether you know what you are talking about or are just copying something from a source. So follow the standard academic writing process. Doing so will make your life much easier, and your grade will reflect that you followed the process.

The tasks in the standard academic writing process include

- Deciding on a topic
- Finding, reading, and taking notes on information
- Sorting information
- Crafting a thesis statement
- Preparing an outline
- Writing a rough draft
- Polishing a final draft

Decide on the Topic

Deciding on the topic of your paper may be the easiest or one of the most difficult steps for you. If your instructor assigns the topic, you can immediately begin your research. If you are responsible for selecting the topic, you have a decision to make.

When you are deciding on a paper topic, keep these three principles in mind:

- **Pick a topic that relates to the class in which the paper has been assigned.** In other words, if you are writing a research paper for an economics class, don't turn in the paper you used for a humanities class unless you can relate it to economics.

- **Make the topic narrow enough to be manageable.** The topic of capitalism, for example, is too broad. The topic of economics during the Reagan administration, however, is much more manageable.

- **Be sure you can find enough information about your topic.** Conduct a few quick searches to make sure that you can find enough information on the subject to write a paper before you waste time on a dead-end topic.

If you are confused about the topic of your research paper (and other issues, such as content and grading), ask your instructor. Instructors sometimes give students ideas on appropriate topics for research papers. If you still aren't sure, seek out an academic coach or tutor for guidance.

You can always look on the Internet to find great topics for research papers. Make sure the site is current. For example, Buzzle.com is a current site that has many research topics to choose from:

www.buzzle.com/articles/research-paper-topics

Suite 101.com is another great site that has tons of tips for topics and help for writing:

www.suite101.com/essay-writing

Take Notes

After reading Chapter 7, "Basic Research Skills," you should know how to find the information you need for your paper. But what do you do with the information you find? You take notes on it.

Taking notes is an important part of research. You will use your notes as the basis of your paper. Follow these tips to taking notes on research:

- Use index cards of different colors so that you have a quick way of identifying their content. If your subject has three main ideas, for example, use three different colors of index cards to take notes.

- Write down major points and pertinent information on your cards. You should also write down where you found the information, using the correct citation format, as you take notes.

- Be accurate and complete in writing down statistics and direct quotations.

- Keep in mind that your paper should consist of no more than 10 to 15 percent quotations. In other words, for the majority of your notes, you have to find the information, read it, analyze it, and put it in your own words.

Sort the Information

After researching your topic and taking notes, the next step is to gather your notes together, sort through them, and organize the information you have gathered, grouping the cards into common subtopics or themes. When you do that, you will begin to see a direction for your paper.

Craft a Thesis Statement

A *thesis statement* is the question you propose to answer in the paper. Remember these basic points about a thesis statement:

- Keep it simple.

- Make it specific by narrowing the subject.

- Make sure that your research supports your thesis statement.

- Ask your professor to approve your thesis statement before you start writing.

Prepare an Outline

The purpose of an outline is to help you think through your topic and to organize the information before you start writing. Your outline should include an introduction, a body, and a conclusion, following these steps:

1. Write an introduction at the top of an outline. Your introduction should include statistics related to the paper or information that will get the attention of those who read your paper. The introduction should also clearly state your thesis and the purpose of your research paper. Why are you writing the paper? Explain briefly the major points you discuss in the paper.

2. Write the body, listing the arguments that support your thesis statement.

3. Write the conclusion, which is a restatement of your thesis statement, summary of your arguments, and an explanation of why you came to this conclusion.

Write a Rough Draft

Do not fall for the temptation to turn in the first version of your research paper. Enter the writing process accepting the fact that the first sentences and paragraphs you write will form a rough draft.

To begin your writing, follow these steps:

1. Copy the introduction from your outline, adding to it as necessary.

2. Read the notes that coincide with the first argument in the body of your outline.

3. Summarize the main point expressed in the notes, and paraphrase or use quotations for every idea you plan to use that relates to this argument.

4. Repeat Steps 1–3 for each of the arguments in your outline.

5. Copy the conclusion from your outline, adjusting it as necessary.

6. Read your paper and check for grammar and spelling errors, using the grammar and spell check features in your word processing program.

7. Have an academic coach or tutor proofread the paper for you.

Polish the Final Draft

When you are satisfied that you have written an interesting introduction, a well-organized body that supports your thesis statement, and a conclusion that recaps the thesis statement in a unique way, you are ready to prepare the final draft. Make sure that you follow these tips:

• Type your paper on a computer. If you are thinking that this is obvious, you might be surprised at how many students turn in handwritten papers.

• Revise your paper, making any changes, running spell check, and having someone proofread it. Use the academic coaching or tutoring service for a proofread.

• Completely reread your paper.

• Go through your paper once more to make sure you didn't miss any errors or grammar mistakes.

After you have finished writing and are ready to print out that final draft, proofread, proofread, proofread. Use spell check and grammar check in the word processing program to check your paper. However, remember words may be spelled correctly, but you could possibly have the wrong word. When you type the word *their* rather than *there*, for example, the computer program won't pick up on the fact that you used the word incorrectly. Also, you may have typed a sentence twice or moved some text around and left some of it behind. Make sure the paper has a nice flow and that it all makes sense.

Some tutors will proofread papers for you and make suggestions on how to improve what you have written. That doesn't mean they are going to rewrite your paper. It means they will guide you by giving you suggestions about grammar, flow, and other details.

Important Issues in Writing Research Papers

Some of the most important issues discussed by professors and those who work in or with academics are cheating, plagiarism, and correct citation format. Once again, rest assured that professors do read your papers, they do pay attention to format, they do know whether you are plagiarizing, and they do know whether you cheat. Read this section carefully, pay attention to which style of citing information is acceptable in your school, and don't plagiarize or cheat. Your success could be drastically affected if you don't take the following information seriously.

Use the Required Style

Make sure that you write the paper in the correct format or style. What is the correct style? It depends on which university or college you attend or the style your instructor prefers. Most universities or colleges and/or instructors state the style that students should use when documenting resources. Find out the style your school and instructor prefer. Most likely, you will use American Psychological Association (APA) or Modern Language Association (MLA) style.

The APA style is the writing style described in the *Publication Manual of the American Psychological Association*. Many other disciplines, such as sociology, business, economics, nursing, social work, and criminology, use the APA style. For more information on this style, see

www.apastyle.org

Scholarly manuscripts and student research papers use the MLA style. It concerns itself with the mechanics of writing, such as punctuation, quotation, and documentation of sources. For more information on MLA, see

www.mla.org/style

Cite Right

After reading an article, you probably will want to refer to it in your paper. You can do this in two ways: You can either directly quote the passage, putting quotation marks around it, or paraphrase it, using your own words to restate the article. You don't want a paper full of quotations, so you should try to paraphrase as much of the information as possible.

Whether you quote or paraphrase others' writings, you need to cite your sources. Most school libraries have a handout, library website, or a book that shows how to cite your sources (also referred to as citations). A citation tells your audience where you found the information in your paper. You must put a brief, specific reference to your source in parentheses at the end of the information and then include a complete citation in a list at the end of your paper.

The following example uses the APA style. It is a short, direct quotation from a book on writing that was written by multiple authors.

> "Any piece of information not set off with quotation marks must be in your own words. Otherwise, even though you name your source, you plagiarize by stealing original phrasing (Reinking, Hart, & von der Osten, 1999, p. 385)."

On the citation page at the end of your paper, you give additional information on where you read that quotation or where you got the information for your paper. Following is the correct format for the citation at the end of the paper:

> Reinking, J., Hart, A., & von der Osten, R. (1999). *Strategies for successful writing* (5th ed.). New Jersey: Prentice-Hall.

This citation indicates that the source of the quotation is a book written by multiple authors.

The formatting of citations varies, depending on the type of resource. Book citations differ from citations for magazine or journal articles, for example. If you are using electronic resources, use the citation format for electronic resources. If you are using paper resources, use the format for paper resources. Get the publication date right. If you aren't sure how to "cite right," get some help. Ask a librarian, an instructor, an academic coach, or a classmate. For further information on correct citation, see the websites mentioned earlier.

Make sure you use the style required by your instructor—for a couple of reasons. First, using the wrong style can seriously affect your paper's grade. Second, correct citations make it easy for your instructor to check your sources.

Writing your paper in the correct format and citing your references correctly does take a little extra time. However, when you have written your paper in the correct format and used the correct citation format once, writing the next paper correctly will be easier and less time-consuming.

Cheating and Plagiarism

With all the things you have going on in your life as a student, sometimes you may be tempted to take the easy way out of writing a paper: You may consider buying a paper or getting someone else to write one for you. Buying a paper already written is blatantly unethical; it is cheating. You are turning in a paper that you didn't write and getting credit for it.

Plagiarism is the act of copying or using other people's words without citing correctly, and it is a significant problem at the university and college level. As a result of plagiarism,

- The person who wrote the original work doesn't get credit.

- The person who plagiarizes gets credit for work that he or she didn't do.

- The person reading the paper may not be able to check the original source and cannot rely on the information.

Many students do not know they are plagiarizing. They may have forgotten where they read the information and just not cite it. They may think that changing a few words around is sufficient. Following are two rules for making sure you don't plagiarize:

- Any fact, idea, or opinion that is not originally yours and not common knowledge must be cited.

- Anything you need to look up is not common knowledge.

Read the articles and books you have gathered for your research. When you decide what information to use, summarize it in your own words. If you are paraphrasing (putting what you read into your own words), make sure that you are writing your own thoughts in your own voice and not just shifting the author's words around or replacing them with syn-onyms. Make sure you let your instructor know where you found your information on the citation page. If an instructor can't locate that infor-mation, you won't get the credit for it.

Trust us. You will feel better if you write your own paper. After you do all the research and write a few papers, *you* are the person who becomes information literate.

Instructors are aware that students can buy papers. They also are aware that students sometimes take shortcuts. Universities and colleges even pay for computer programs and subscription services for faculty to use that will tell them whether a student bought a paper or plagiarized some-one else's work. Please trust us when we say that most instructors will read your papers, they will check your resources, and they will know if you cheated or plagiarized. Don't take the chance of getting a zero on a paper or flunking a class. Do your own work.

Conclusion

Writing a research paper is not an easy task. We hate to use the old cliché of "practice makes perfect," but it is true. The more papers you write by following the correct process and learning the correct cita-tion format, the more successful you will be as a student. Do your best, remember to use your support system, and get help if you need it. By doing your own work and doing it correctly, you will feel more positive about yourself, and your grades will reflect your success.

Best Practices: Writing Research Papers

Do

- Do know what style or format should be used in writing your paper.
- Do use the correct resources subscribed to by your institution for mining information.
- Do use current information.
- Do follow all of the steps of the academic writing process when you write a paper.
- Do ask your academic coach or tutor to proof your paper.

(continued)

(continued)

- Do write in third person and check that your verb tenses are consistent.

- Do know how to "cite right," using the required style so that your paper is formatted correctly.

Don't

- Don't plagiarize or use someone else's paper.

- Don't write your paper without doing your research first.

- Don't procrastinate writing your paper.

Assignment 8.1: Explore Types of Research Papers

In this assignment, you learn more about the types of research papers you may be required to write. Complete these steps:

1. Go to the Purdue OWL (Online Writing Lab) at

   http://owl.english.purdue.edu/owl

2. Click on Subject Specific Writing. You will see a listing of different types of research papers.

3. In the space provided below or in a separate document, list three different types of papers and give a brief description of each. You may have to click on the different types to get a description of what those papers should contain.

   First type: _____

   _____

   _____

   _____

Second type: _____

_____

_____

_____

Third type: _____

_____

_____

_____

Assignment 8.2: Review Writing Mechanics

In this assignment, you brush up your writing skills by doing some writing exercises. Complete these steps:

1. Go to the OWL writing lab at:

   http://owl.english.purdue.edu/owl

2. Click on OWL Exercises.

3. Click on Grammar Exercises. Click on one of the topics and complete one of the exercises.

4. Click on Sentence Structure. Click on one of the topics and complete one of the exercises.

CHAPTER 9

Synergy

"One horse can pull 2 tons, but 2 horses can pull 42 tons."

George MacDonald

Synergy is defined as the combined or cooperative action of two or more agents, groups, or parts that together increase each other's effectiveness. Just as the quote often attributed to George MacDonald states, we can accomplish much more when we have synergy, or help, than we are capable of doing alone. It is a truth that two heads are better than one. In fact, two heads can often synergize and do many times the work of one person, just as the horse analogy indicates. A critical secret for student success is recognizing the fact that you need others' help to be a winner.

Relationship Styles

What is your style of relating to others? Are you a Lone Ranger? Or do you recognize the rich resources your cohorts can be for you? Do you accept and use all that others in your life can offer you? How savvy are you about creating and using relationships effectively?

The Lone Ranger

Are you a person who usually goes it alone? Do you get assignments and feel you have to tackle them by yourself? Do you feel uncomfortable asking people to assist you when you are stuck? Then this chapter is for you.

Even the Lone Ranger wasn't really alone. He had his trusty sidekick, Tonto, and his horse, Silver. Students aren't alone either. Despite the fact that you may initially feel alone, classmates, instructors, technical support personnel, student services mentors, and a host of others are available to assist you—if you seek their help. And the best way to synergize with these people is to ask!

Cohorts

You need support from others in your classes. With a little know-how and practice, you can find emotional and intellectual bonding in your class. But how?

When you feel as if no one is out there, reach out to instructors or other students. All instructors have office hours. If you can't find a convenient time to see an instructor, send e-mail or leave a voice message. And remember this: Other students probably feel as alone as you feel. Ask for classmates' e-mail addresses or phone numbers. Don't be afraid to get connected to instructors or fellow classmates. (If you are an online student, you probably will find that people open up even more because they have a sense of anonymity.)

The Others

Many students readily recognize that fellow students and instructors related to their education offer synergism. However, few see the people directly in front of them—family, friends, and coworkers, just to name a few—in this way.

Once again, ask for help. Whether you are asking family and friends to help care for your children, elderly parents, pets, or other responsibilities, ask. People in your circle can make your life easier while you're getting an education; use them. Let someone pick up your kids. Let someone cook for you. Let someone help you.

Can you exchange services? Perhaps you can type fast. Can you exchange typing a friend's paper for help with child care? You don't have to write the paper; just type what he or she has already written. When you understand the power of synergy, you know that no matter what problem might occur, you can ask for help, and a solution will be found. Ask.

The Win-Win of Synergy

Many of us hesitate to ask for help. However, on more than one occasion after people have helped us, they have told us that, by requesting their help, we have actually helped them. We cannot guarantee reciprocal help, but we want you to see the opportunity your asking for help gives others.

Synergy involves the simple concept of sharing. Sharing what you are learning helps reinforce what you have learned. Be willing to help another classmate (not cheating, but student mentoring). Become involved with fellow classmates. Ask them what they are getting out of the course, and you will find valuable perspectives. Interact with other students so that you can gain new, fresh ideas important to your studies.

How can you synergize your life? The following sections discuss these methods of activating synergy in your life:

- Be assertive.

- Keep an open mind.

- Be personal.

- Network and share.

- Don't bail.

Be Assertive

Students should speak up and take initiative when they are having difficulties. If you are an online student and the Internet technology is not working, for example, let someone know. Getting online should not be difficult. Don't waste time trying to figure out that which you do not know. Many schools have free 24/7 tech help and online tutoring available. Find out and keep the tech help number and e-mail address near your work desk. Remember, the squeaky wheel gets the grease.

The same can be said for on-campus students who are working in a computer lab. If you are having trouble getting a printer or an application program to work, find someone who works in the lab, look for an academic coach, or even ask someone else you see working in the lab.

It's also important to remember that people can't read minds. If you don't ask, others can't help you. If you don't know whom to ask, pick someone and ask whom he or she would ask for answers.

Keep an Open Mind

Be open to learning new things. Just because you haven't used the applications in your school computer labs or some type of media doesn't mean you can't learn how to do so. If you aren't sure how to get started, ask for help.

After you have asked for help, you may get some seemingly off-the-wall answers to your questions. Don't immediately reject any answer until you prove it to be of no help. Ideas and opinions are not necessarily good or bad, just different and within the realm of possibility. Many great inventions came from seemingly off-the-wall ideas and answers. The Wright brothers, Thomas Edison, and Albert Einstein are just a few people who had or were given off-the-wall answers that were not rejected. Thank goodness for that!

Be Personal

Tip: If you are an online student, use the other learners' names in class discussions. Also, reference the topic and sign your name to your posts. Doing so makes threads much easier to follow. Find out how your instructor prefers to be addressed and then use that name.

Successful students will tell you to address people by name or title. Being personal in this way is particularly important in the classroom environment when you are asking and answering questions, especially if you are e-mailing a question. Many people assume that most e-mail messages are junk mail and automatically delete them. However, when you send an e-mail with the person's name and/or title, he or she is much more likely to answer you.

Network and Share

Networking involves seeking professional relationships with your classmates, instructors, and school staff. Networks provide strength and resources.

Readily sharing tips and suggestions for success is often referred to as the "glue" in networking relationships. You don't have to reinvent the wheel. Others may have already invented it or know where to find it. Reach out to them and synergize.

Don't Bail

If you are not doing as well as you hoped, stay in touch with your instructor and the class. Ask your instructor whether academic coaches or tutors are available for your class and ask for their contact information. Most tutoring services offered by the school are free. Ask whether any of your classmates would be willing to assist you. (You can offer to pay for the call if you are an online student, but they might help you through e-mail.)

Above all, ask for help when you do not understand a concept. Instructors cannot read your mind (at least, most cannot). If you have questions, ask! Most course content builds concept upon concept. You might miss out on an entire concept because you failed to ask for clarification. Successful students advise others to use all the resources available.

Above all else, don't quit. If you are doing something you believe will make your life better, don't quit. A popular saying you will find to be true among your classmates and many others states, "If you have never felt like quitting, then you really weren't running the race." The point is that nearly everyone has felt like quitting at one time or another. If you haven't, you probably aren't even running the race. Don't give up. Walk or crawl if you have to, but finish the race. It's a race you started. It's a race worth finishing!

> **Tip:** If you are an online student, see whether your online class has a built-in electronic library and search engines available to you. This could be a library Web page or could include electronic resources such as ProQuest, NetLibrary, and others you learned about in Chapter 7, "Basic Research Skills." Most schools do have such resources, and you will get your own password to use them.

Synergy for Online Students

Unlike a traditional class, an online class depends upon e-mail and bulletin board postings for all class and instructor interactions. Checking into your class frequently will ensure that you stay informed of the important things going on in class.

When you never see another person's face, it is easy to feel isolated; however, you are not alone. Be sure to ask questions if you need clarification. Though you cannot go to your instructor's office in person, most online instructors have office hours, where you can reach them in real time by phone or e-mail. E-mail often provides you with quick responses day or night and even on the weekend, when most students are doing their homework. Being an online student is far from being isolated or cut off—unless you choose to make it that way. You just have to communicate in a different way online.

Learning online is a different type of learning experience than traditional classrooms provide. Be open to learning through a new medium and try not to accept preconceived ideas about learning online.

Conclusion

Synergy is defined as the combined or cooperative action of two or more agents, groups, or parts that together increase each other's effectiveness. And now that you know what synergy is and how valuable it can be, you have no reason for not implementing this best practice. You can harness the energy of others through synergy, which is essentially a principle of success that states, "You should never go it alone." You need to allow others to participate in your process and in your life, dreams, and goals. Your effects won't just double; they'll increase exponentially. Try using synergy, and you will see many miracles come to fruition in your life when you work with others and let them help you.

Best Practices: Synergy

Do

- Do seek help from your classmates. They are in the same boat as you. Row together and make sure you ask where the restroom is.

- Do seek help from your family, friends, and coworkers. These people are often initially overlooked, but they want to help you succeed. When you succeed, so do they.

- Do see asking as win-win. Those from whom you seek help are often helped themselves.

- Do be assertive. The squeaky wheel gets the grease. Some great online student advice is to step up and speak up.

- Do have an open mind. You may get some unique advice when you ask for it, but don't immediately discount any idea as bunk.

- Do be personal. E-mails should always begin with the person's name. The sweetest sound (and sight) in the whole world is your own name, whether spoken or typed.

- Do share and network. Your class is a great place to network. If you don't share, we guarantee you won't be able to network.

- Do ask about tutoring services. Many online schools are using www.smarthinking.com. Check it out.

Don't

- Don't go it alone. If you do, it will be a very tough road to graduation—much tougher than it has to be.

- Don't be afraid to ask. FEAR stands for "False Expectations Appearing Real." If you are afraid to ask, you will be afraid to succeed.

- Don't quit. Never give up. It's as easy and as difficult as that!

Assignment 9.1: Conduct a Web Hunt for Synergistic Ways to Win

Go to the following websites and find three ways you can increase synergy in your own life. Write them in the space provided and be prepared to share them with your class.

www.profitadvisors.com/synergize.shtml

www.adventureassoc.com/resources/team-work-skills/teamwork-skills.html

(continued)

(continued)

1. _____

_____

2. _____

_____

3. _____

_____

Assignment 9.2: Create Synergistic Networking

Practice the principles in this chapter by completing the following steps.

1. Find out and record the names and e-mail addresses of three of your classmates:

Name: _____

E-mail: _____

Name: _____

E-mail: _____

Name _____

E-mail: _____

2. Write down three ways you can use synergy to help you succeed in school:

   1. _____

   _____

   2. _____

   _____

   3. _____

   _____

CHAPTER 10

Motivation

"The secret of getting ahead is getting started."

Often attributed to Mark Twain

It has been said that you need to be a self-starter to be successful. In any classroom situation, being a self-starter will only enhance your success. If you don't consider yourself a self-starter, don't despair. You can learn how to take action and become self-motivated. *Motivation* is a willingness to perform a certain action (such as taking online classes or enrolling in college) for a real or perceived reward (such as a college degree, a better career, more money). When you take action and create reward statements, you will find it just as easy to motivate yourself to complete your coursework as it is to motivate yourself to go to the movies.

Success Principles in Motivation

A common misconception is that people are born self-motivated. The truth is that you must choose to be motivated. The success principle of motivation is based on the premise of wanting to do something.

The statement "I have to start classes this fall so that I can graduate and get a better job" and the statement "I want to start classes this fall so that I can graduate and get a better job" look very similar, but they are *not* the same. The only thing we all "have to" do in life is die some day. Everything else is a choice.

By replacing the words "have to" with the words "want to," you prime your subconscious to process your tasks as desirable and motivating. In other words, you create a reward system linked to your behavior regardless of whether you truly "want to."

Assignment 10.1: Change the Messages You Send to Your Subconscious

Complete the following tasks.

1. List five tasks that you don't want to do related to college.

   _____

   _____

   _____

   _____

   _____

2. Rewrite the five tasks, beginning with the words, "I want to" and ending with the reward you expect to receive.

   _____

   _____

   _____

   _____

   _____

3. Repeat the list in step 2 every day for 21 days. Soon you will find yourself motivated enough to become a successful, self-starting student.

An example of this assignment for an online student follows:

1. I **want to** learn how to use the computer so I can be successful in online classes and get a degree that will earn me more money.

2. I **want to** spend 10 hours a week in each of my online classes so I can maintain at least a 3.5 grade point average and have the best chance of getting into law school.

3. I **want to** organize my office/computer area and always keep it neat and clean so I can maximize my online class efficiency and effectiveness.

4. I **want to** take a typing course so I can be more efficient in online classes and spend more time with my family.

5. I **want to** take the online orientation course before I take my first class so that I can be more proficient and successful.

The reality may be that you feel you "have to" learn to use the computer, or spend 10 hours a week in each online class, or organize and keep your office/computer area neat and clean, or take a typing class, or take an online orientation course. However, by telling yourself that you "want to" do these things and justifying them with appropriate rewards and outcomes, you are creating a fertile atmosphere for self-motivation. You will notice a difference.

Visualize the Reward

Find your desire in succeeding with your classes. Get in touch with the "big picture." Go to the future in your mind and ask, "How will my life look different on the outside when I successfully complete my classes?" For example, can you see yourself in your desired career as a powerful, highly successful employee or entrepreneur? Perhaps your life is filled with multiple new possibilities and choices for yourself and others.

The reason to visualize the reward is that learning can seem like a maze you "have to" go through to get the cheese (the reward). The goal, of course, is to visualize the cheese and *want* to go through the maze. If you focus on the cheese, you will become inspired and self-motivated before and during the journey.

Overcome Motivation Roadblocks

Inevitably, you will run into roadblocks in getting your education. Yet it has been said, "The only difference between stepping stones and stumbling blocks is how they are used." We believe this statement to be true, and so do hundreds of successful students. In fact, some of the most common stumbling blocks, such as time limitations and disorganization, can easily be remedied. By using the tools and best practices from Chapter 4, "Organization," and Chapter 11, "Time and Energy Management," you can create a new path around, over, or underneath the roadblocks in your academic journey. The secrets to success identified in these chapters will empower you when you get stuck or off-track so that you can get quickly back on track and moving toward your goals.

Build on Small Victories

Get familiar with the class structure and your instructor. You need to learn how to navigate and become acclimated to your surroundings. The more time you spend getting comfortable in the platform now, the more time and energy you will have available to devote to succeeding in your actual course work in the future.

When you have successfully completed a class, pat yourself on the back. You can use this small victory to build significant motivation to propel you through your course curriculum.

Balance Your Life

Balance is another identified key to success as a student. We must not underestimate its importance primarily because of the frequency with which students focus solely on motivating themselves to complete courses and their degree, while neglecting other areas of their lives.

To prevent this "tunnel" motivation, you might want to map out how you are doing in the key areas of school, work, health, family, finances, spirituality, and social life. If you ignore any one of these areas, you will get out of balance, potentially sabotaging your success, as time management expert Dr. Donald E. Wetmore points out. As he says in his online articles about saving time, "If you fail to take time for your health now, you will need to take time for illness later."

Successful students remind others to get plenty of rest and eat well. You are fueling the engine from which your work flows. It is vital to fuel your engine so you can be excited and interested in the material, instead of waiting for others to make it interesting for you.

Surround Yourself with Winners

Surround yourself with people who want you to win and believe in you. Keep in mind that it takes 11 positive people to undo the negative energy of 1 negative person, so stay away from negative, fault-finding people as much as possible. They will systematically take your enthusiasm and motivation from you. Stay strong and surround yourself with people who also want you to succeed.

Instructors are sometimes unable to motivate students. However, those of you who are self-motivated and self-disciplined have a unique benefit that provides you with the independence and opportunity to work at your own pace. Being self-reliant gives you the flexibility you need to be successful.

Motivation Versus Enthusiasm

Hundreds of successful motivational speakers travel the country each year. They are paid well by a variety of corporations and social organizations to motivate employees to perform, produce, and invent. Many companies invite the speakers back year after year because of the results attributed to their motivating the people who attend.

The reality of motivational speakers is that very few actually motivate people. Rather, they create an atmosphere of enthusiasm similar to that of a sports pep rally. They often talk about changing the world, and indeed we have been to many motivational seminars and felt inspired after the speech. However, that feeling or desire to change the world quickly faded as the hours moved past.

The reason for this phenomenon is that most motivational speakers are actually "enthusiasm" speakers. They create a short-term intense feeling of change, creativity, and drive. However, unless the speaker can connect individually with each person in the audience, the short-term enthusiasm will never transform into long-term self-motivation and manifest into action.

It is easy to feel enthusiastic about succeeding in your classes after reading this book. In fact, many students will be raring to go before completing all the chapters. But completing a degree is more than a short-winded sprint that requires only temporary enthusiasm. A college degree is reached only through perseverance and self-motivation. And if you are self-motivated, you can earn your degree in less time.

Self-motivation results from a conscious perceived reward or benefit attached to behavior and performance changes. It's the typical carrot-in-front-of-the-horse analogy. However, if the horse doesn't get a bite of the carrot every now and again, he will quit walking. This is precisely the stance successful students take for generating self-motivation. Each successful assignment, quiz, or project is like taking a bite from the carrot in front of them. It motivates them to walk a few steps further until the course is successfully completed. A few more carrots—make that classes—and you have the benefit of a college degree.

Conclusion

After you read this chapter, take time to do a personal inventory and decide whether you can be self-motivated (largely a decision based on habits rather than an innate behavior). You are in charge of your own life. You choose whether to apply the principles of creating an atmosphere of motivation in your life. If you cannot choose to change your habits to motivate yourself, success may more difficult. You will be working against yourself. Learn to go with the flow.

Best Practices: Motivation

Do

- Do visualize your reward. Focus on your goals of taking college classes. It's easier to become motivated when you use visualization.

- Do have realistic expectations. Expectations of rewards for behavior are what drive motivation. Make sure your expectations are realistic and not just a pipe dream.

- Do move around motivation roadblocks. Use organization (Chapter 4) and time and energy management (Chapter 11) secrets to turn stumbling blocks into stepping stones.

- Do balance your life motivation. Include your motivation for good health, happiness, and family harmony.

- Do surround yourself with winners. Water rises to its own level. Surround yourself with winners and positive people, and you will become one, too.

- Do say "I want to" rather than "I have to." Remember this key success principle as you do the things that are less than fun.

- Do build on small victories. Use victories of completing an assignment or the orientation class to motivate yourself to complete your degree.

Don't

- Don't confuse enthusiasm with motivation. Enthusiasm is short-term excitement; motivation is long-term energy tied to realistic expectations and rewards.

- Don't lose your motivation focus. Periodically review your goals and their associated rewards.

- Don't blame others for your lack of motivation. You are in charge of yourself, your thoughts, and your actions.

Assignment 10.2: Find Motivation Tips on the Web

Go to the following websites or choose your own through a search engine:

www.mindtools.com/pages/article/newLDR_57.htm

www.goal-setting-college.com/motivation/5-tips-to-daily-motivation

Find three tools or tips you could use to motivate yourself or others in a constructive manner. Write them in the space provided and be prepared to share these with your class.

1. _____

_____

2. _____

_____

3. _____

_____

CHAPTER 11

Time and Energy Management

"The only reason for time is so that everything doesn't happen at once."

Albert Einstein

Remember that you are accountable for managing your time. Accept full responsibility for your schedule. If you blame others for what you seemingly "have to do," your life will stay stuck in a helpless mode. To move to the life you want, you must take control and responsibility for your time. If you need to pick up your children, for example, recognize that that is your choice, and you will have more energy if you acknowledge that reality. It is your life and your opportunity to succeed or fail. You get to decide. Remind yourself of this concept on a daily basis.

The Keys to Time Management

Do you know how to manage your time, or do you always feel as if you're playing catch-up? How can you find the time to do all the things you need to do? We have some simple but powerful keys that can help you unlock the door to hours in your days.

Plan Ahead

You want to rid yourself of the notion that "there is always tomorrow." If something is going to be accomplished, it will be because you made it happen, either consciously or by default. Planning your time leaves less up to fate and chance. Decide on a plan to allocate and balance your time: family, job, school, and social activities. Decide what you want and need to do each week and plot it all out. Without a plan, you can easily get distracted and off-track.

We have this note of caution: When planning ahead, don't overplan. Allow some things to resolve themselves—and, trust us, they will. When you preplan everything, you put life in a box. Quite frankly, life is much more fluid than that. You want to allow opportunities for "aha" experiences to work in your life, and for that to happen, you need some breathing room. So have a plan, but don't become so rigid that you block out the easier or more enjoyable ways to accomplish your goals.

Learn When to Say "Yes" and When to Say "No"

Be true to your word. Say "No" when you mean "No." Say "Yes" when you mean and want to say "Yes." To maintain balance in your life, you will want to say "No" to some things. However, you also will want to say "Yes" on occasion to gain new experiences and perspectives that may directly benefit your learning experience. If you say "Yes" too often and spread yourself too thin, you will reduce the energy allotted for your educational goals. Remember, guilt goes away; resentment does not.

Avoid Procrastination

Procrastination is habitually putting off things that you should be doing. If that sounds like something you do, pay special attention to this section. There is hope.

Avoid procrastination at all costs! It can make you miss deadlines and create an unpleasant experience. Procrastinating can also cause a great deal of stress, which actually inhibits learning. When you are concentrating on catching up, odds are good that you are not absorbing the information in class, which leads to other problems down the road.

One key to avoiding procrastination is to stop using the words "have to." The words you tell yourself affect your behavior, so you need to be careful with the words you use. When you say "have to," you start the procrastination process. Your subconscious starts thinking of ways that it does not "have to." You end up fighting yourself, and the procrastinating process begins.

Instead, as you learned in Chapter 10, "Motivation," you should tell yourself the reasons you **want to** do something. You want to study to pass the test. If you pass the test, you pass the class. If you pass the class, you are closer to receiving your degree. You **want to** do your work now so you will have free time later. You want to; you do not have to. Remember that you don't have to do anything but die—almost everything else is a choice.

The second key to avoiding procrastination is to not allow others to take over your study time. One way to do this is to have a set study time. Your family and friends will be less likely to sidetrack you if they know your study schedule in advance.

On the flip side, you don't always want to neglect others, either. Rather, try making a win-win arrangement for all concerned. You can do this. Reward your family and yourself for keeping to your study schedule. When you study at the times designated and you do well on your exams or assignments, treat yourself to extra time with friends or family or do something fun for an hour or two. You can take in that movie you wanted to see or take the kids to the park.

Establish a Routine

Another reason you should study at a certain time on a regular basis is that doing so trains your brain to know that now it is time to focus and absorb knowledge. Establish a dedicated time for your studies and develop the habit of doing your studying at a certain time on certain days so your brain will become ready to absorb knowledge.

Prioritize

Another time management secret to being a successful learner is the ability to prioritize. People who don't know how to prioritize become procrastinators. A big part of effective time management is being able to set priorities so you can keep on track with everything you have to do surrounding your responsibilities inside and outside of being a student. Even if you are busy, you can schedule your tasks, depending on their priority in your life. You should align your efforts with your goals and your life purpose. Doing so will cause you to put more priority on the important tasks rather than just the urgent ones.

Use Lists

In order to prioritize, you need to make decisions about what are your "babies"—that is, the tasks that are most important to you. You can choose from among many ways to do this. One is to make a list of daily things you want to get accomplished and then mark or circle the ones that are essential to do that day. Then schedule the days and times in which to do your work and keep them as interruption-free as possible. This way, you give your coursework a high priority in your life and take it more seriously. Establishing your coursework as a priority will make you more successful than if you just sit down to study when you have "free" time.

You can make a separate list for personal items or make one list with all the goals of the day. You can also make a list at the end of your workday for the next day. That way, you can rest knowing that you will tend to details the next day with nothing being overlooked or forgotten. Keep in mind that, no matter how you slice it, you have 24 hours in a day to work with. Consider limiting your list to 10 items, with the 5 most important highlighted, and a timeframe for completion. Determine the activities in your day that are time wasters and eliminate them.

Another way to prioritize is to identify your top three or four items for the day and tend to them, rather than making a long list of less important things. Keep in mind that if getting the dry cleaning on the way home will increase the peace at home, that item might be worth putting on the list.

Some experts suggest making three lists: One that includes your long-term success goals; one that has urgent, but not as important things you want to accomplish; and one more list of things that are nice to do or have, but only if you have the time. The warning here from successful learners is to *not* spend so much time making lists prioritizing daily events and scheduling that you don't have enough time for your coursework.

Keep your to-do lists near your study area so that you can cross items off as you complete them. Humans are teleological: Once we make a goal, we seek to do it like a heat-seeking missile. In other words, if you consciously think about it, your thoughts and actions will gravitate toward your goals. Harness this aspect of your being.

Furthermore, you may want to put another list near you for your worries, but write at the top that you are shelving them or letting a power higher than you deal with them. We know people who write their problems on a list. When they go home at the end of the day, they leave the list in the mailbox so they can focus on their family. Then they pick up the list in the morning and take it to work with them. This action is symbolic of letting go of things that you have no control over so you can focus on your goals, whether that is family time or studying.

Spend Your Time on the Right Things

An important part of prioritizing is learning how to "do the right things right." It is good to be efficient, but if you are being efficient at things that are not taking you anywhere, then really, what have you accomplished? Not much. Rather, the best practice is to learn how to be efficient at effective things.

Your time is valuable. Put a price on it. Don't step over dollars to pick up dimes. Don't spend your time and energy on useless time wasters. Become less rigid about what you believe you need to accomplish. Just because you have always done something a certain way does not mean that it is the most effective, efficient method. Keep your eyes open to shortcuts.

Hang around people who seem to be "doing the right things right" and ask them how they plan and strategize their time and life. Adapt new, effective techniques in your life. If you don't, it is easy to become a "busyaholic" who is not producing much but looks busy and feels overextended. Many people are in the rut of rushing around in a frenzy and accomplishing very little. Yet their energy is spent, and they get up and do the same thing the next day.

To prevent the "busyaholic" time management practice, you should work and study smarter, not harder. You can follow the 80/20 rule. In other words, 20 percent of your efforts produce 80 percent of the results. For more information, do an Internet search on "80/20 rule of time management."

Pamela J. Vacarro wrote an interesting article on the 80/20 rule for *Family Practice Management* (a journal of the American Academy of Family

Physicians), which is available at the following website:

www.aafp.org/fpm/20000900/76the8.html

Bruce Keener describes Stephen Covey's tools for the process of prioritizing at the following website:

www.dkeener.com/keenstuff/priority.html

Map Your Time

One suggestion for making your own time schedule is to take a piece of poster board and tack it to your wall. On this board, mark spaces or time slots and map out a schedule that you would like to follow. You can use hours or half-hour time slots for a busy schedule. Include commitments such as soccer games and doctor's appointments as well as classes, work, meals, and driving time. This method enables others in your life to know what you would like to be doing or are doing on any particular day at any time.

When you look at what you have scheduled, you can now ask yourself if you have enough time. Most likely your answer is that you do not. What you have done is set forth a map to use as a guide. Don't be a perfectionist about this. Sometimes you should work toward perfection, but this is not one of those times. Use your time schedule as a goal. See whether you can find a way to take a few minutes off one thing and add the extra time to the things that mean the most to you. Find ways to combine activities. For example, listen to taped lectures while you exercise or while driving.

Energy Management

We each have the same 24 hours to work with in a day. So how come some people move mountains while others have a hard time just getting up in the morning? Managing your energy is just as, or even more important than, managing your time. You could have all the time in the world to write a paper, but if you don't manage your energy, you might not make it happen.

Learn how to harness the times of day when you have more energy, and let yourself rest or exercise occasionally, too. Capitalize on your body rhythms and identify your biological prime time. Schedule your study time when you are at peak energy for it, and allow for breaks. Another suggestion is to schedule your long meetings right before lunch or at the end of the day.

Learn how to say no to energy wasters, be it surfing the Internet or taking on one more commitment because you felt guilty. You owe it to yourself to be a champion for yourself. No one else is going to come in and readjust your life to help you make time to finish your degree. You need to decide that you are worth it and therefore you will devote your energy (and time) to making it happen. There will be plenty of time in the future to volunteer for another committee. You can't afford to burn out now. You need all of the energy you can muster to get the job done. Remind yourself that you are worth this college degree each and every day.

Furthermore, people who aren't doing what you are doing may not become your cheerleaders. They might secretly harbor a hope you will quit (they will be there to cheer you up!), and you might hear all sorts of talk, such as

> *"Single parents need to focus on raising their kids, not get a degree—do that later, your kids are only young once."*

Or

> *"You're not much fun anymore. You don't make time for us."*

You will need to take a long-range look at your goals and go back to the reason why you enrolled in college in the first place. Look around, most or many of your classmates have as many or more commitments, stresses, and struggles as you do, and guess what? They are doing it! Not perfectly, but they are doing it, and you can too if you manage your time and energy.

Ten Time Management Principles for Online Learners

Time management is a must if you expect to stay focused from week to week and have time to stay on top of the studies that you must manage for yourself as an online student. Online students cannot just procrastinate on projects, quizzes, and term papers (although it's not advisable for traditional onsite students to do that, either). Most online courses close the week with a grace day or two and make missed assignments or quizzes unavailable. This time lag or "grace day" allows the instructor to grade your assignments. The familiar adage, "If you snooze, you lose" comes to mind in the online environment.

Just as you are unique, with your own priorities, commitments, and responsibilities, your ideal way to manage your time and energy is going to reflect your individuality. Your goal is to have a relationship with your time and your energy that feels meaningful and valuable and enables you to meet the obligations of your professional life, family, and social life. You also want to have the time to take care of your most valuable asset—your health.

Although we do not have a one-size-fits-all time management formula, we do offer some basic principles you can adapt to your special circumstances:

- **Principle 1: Your most important tool in an online class is your computer.** You should use this time management tool to your advantage. One of the most important things to download and print is the online course syllabus—essentially, the contract between the instructor and you. The syllabus usually includes a summary of assignments, quizzes, tests, projects or term papers, case studies, and grading policies. Successful online students also download their weekly assignments and lectures and print them so they can work when they are away from "class" or the computer.

- **Principle 2: Do it right the first time.** When completing assignments, quizzes, and so on, successful online students take the time to make sure they are following instructions correctly, saving themselves the time they would have spent redoing the work. Conversely, if they make mistakes, they don't beat themselves up. Rather, they learn from their mistakes and move forward.

- **Principle 3: Not all things are worth doing perfectly.** For example, typing your grocery list and spending hours making sure that you have listed everything you might need before you leave the house is not a good use of your time. Make a "good enough" grocery list and get on with it. Getting your work done is so much better than not doing it at all due to some unforeseen crisis.

Furthermore, communicate with your instructors if you are in a crisis; more often than not, they will work with you.

- **Principle 4: Create a plan to allocate and balance your family, job, school, and social activities.** Asynchronous classes allow students to decide when and where to study and log in. Therefore, you want to make a time management plan that has enough wiggle room to allow for daily changes or emergencies.

- **Principle 5: Schedule some recreation.** Your goal should be to maintain a balanced life while taking online courses. Take inventory of the priorities in your life and where you feel you need to adjust. You can still have the life you seek while taking online classes.

- **Principle 6: Set designated times on your calendar to go online each day and week.** Remember that little bits and chunks of time add up. The recommendations for participation per week for most online courses average 8 to 15 hours. Go into your online class at every opportunity, even if you have only 5 to 10 minutes. You probably make time to check your personal e-mail several times a day, so start checking your online course e-mail every day as well. Jump on the discussion boards, if only for a few minutes. Some online classes even require that you post on different days of the week in order to obtain full participation points. Expecting to pull an all-nighter until the work is done is setting yourself up for a journey that may not be pleasant for your loved ones or you. With a little planning, the journey can be an enjoyable one.

- **Principle 7: Do your work when you are supposed to do it.** It is easy to procrastinate online and to fool yourself into thinking that nobody knows whether you log in or turn in your assignments. Of course, the reality is that electronic tracking systems are exceedingly accurate. The computer platforms can track when you log in, where you go in the class, what you submit, and how long you work in each area. Do not be fooled by thinking you can hide in an online class.

- **Principle 8: Do something in the right direction.** Sometimes just getting started is the key to breaking the procrastination habit. One tool you can use is to do the one thing you do not want to do for five minutes. This is known as the 5-Minute Rule. This action will often be enough to break the procrastination. Set a timer and work for just five minutes, and then see if you can do five more. Often you just need to get started in order to succeed.

- **Principle 9: Do the things you don't want to do first.** Get them out of the way. You can use typical procrastinating behaviors, such as checking personal e-mail, playing Internet games, or getting a snack, as rewards for doing some work in your class. This way, your typical procrastinator behaviors become an incentive rather than a way to avoid working. If you fall behind, try to get back on track as soon as possible.

- **Principle 10: Accept the fact that your attendance will most likely be at odd hours.** Regardless, you should make an attendance routine in order to create a new and positive habit.

Conclusion

In this chapter, we have presented several methods of effective and efficient time and energy management strategies from the comments of hundreds of successful students. Hopefully, you will find one or more of these best practices helpful in your success. However, do not try to apply *all* of these time management practices. You don't want to make scheduling, prioritizing, and other time management activities monopolize precious time that you need to complete coursework. Initially, it may take a few hours to develop a time management plan. But a good rule to follow while you are taking classes is to spend less than two hours a week organizing your time.

Best Practices: Time Management

Do

- Do allow time to absorb what you are learning. The ability to grasp a new learned thought will lead to a better understanding.

- Do make working on your class a habit. If you write down on a calendar when you need to submit something online, you will not have to worry about forgetting whether you went online.

- Do something each day for your class. That way, you aren't stressed by last-minute deadlines.

- Do get other essential non–course-related tasks out of the way before studying so that you aren't worried about all the things you have to do in addition to studying.

- Do take a break, drink plenty of water, and relax. If you don't, you'll actually take longer to do the same amount of work.

- Do cancel, postpone, or decrease other commitments to free time for your courses. It pays off in better grades, increased knowledge, and less stress.

- Do start with the most difficult assignment. Your energy level needs to be at its highest for success with these sorts of tasks.

Don't

- Don't spend too much time organizing and scheduling your week. Don't walk over dollars to pick up dimes.

- Don't implement all time management techniques. Picking one or two that fit your life is sufficient.

- Don't fret over things for which you don't have time. Prioritize, delegate, and do what you can. Remember it is all about progress, not perfection. Perfectionism is not a success tool.

Assignment 11.1: Personal Time and Energy Survey

Most experts suggest using the personal time survey tool if you truly want to have more "time" in your life. For 24 hours, plot your time on this chart so you can find the time wasters and holes that are wasting your precious energy. In the long run, this simple activity can significantly change your life. You will gain an amazing awareness because so many time management habits are unconscious. By having an awareness of how you spend your time and energy, you can start shifting that energy to effective and efficient activities.

(continued)

(continued)

Hours		Hours	
6:00 am		6:00 pm	
6:30 am		6:30 pm	
7:00 am		7:00 pm	
7:30 am		7:30 pm	
8:00 am		8:00 pm	
8:30 am		8:30 pm	
9:00 am		9:00 pm	
9:30 am		9:30 pm	
10:00 am		10:00 pm	
10:30 am		10:30 pm	
11:00 am		11:00 pm	
11:30 am		11:30 pm	
NOON		MIDNIGHT	
12:30 pm		12:30 am	
1:00 pm		1:00 am	
1:30 pm		1:30 am	
2:00 pm		2:00 am	
2:30 pm		2:30 am	
3:00 pm		3:00 am	
3:30 pm		3:30 am	
4:00 pm		4:00 am	
4:30 pm		4:30 am	
5:00 pm		5:00 am	
5:30 pm		5:30 am	

After completing the personal time survey, it is often best to prioritize your schedule by looking a week ahead. When planning your week's schedule, include all your activities and look ahead to the following week. If the week ahead is jam-packed with deadlines and appointments that cannot be rescheduled, but this week is a light load, schedule time to do at least 50 percent of next week's studying this week. Also, when the week is over, examine what parts of the classes took more time than you expected and allocate more time for those areas for the next week's schedule.

Assignment 11.2: Describe Your Perfect Day

Now that you know what your day is really like and you have given thought to how you can construct it, you can take it a step further and raise the stakes a bit by doing this assignment. We are making this assignment because we believe the success tool that says, "If you can think it up, you can have it—with some effort, of course."

Think about and write a description of what a typical day would look like if your concerns or problems were solved. Keep in mind that the details are significant here. We are asking you to make up a true story. If you make it vague, then you will get a vague life, probably not what you truly desire. Answer the following questions in the space provided:

1. When do you do your work? To answer, think about when you are most energetic, happy, and excited about life. Are you a morning person, or is your energy better in the afternoon or evening?

   _____

   _____

2. Where do you work—in an office, cubicle, or your home? How long of a commute do you have?

   _____

   _____

(continued)

(continued)

3. What type of a business do you work for—how large or what type of organization?

_____

_____

4. What kind of a boss or supervisor do you have, or are you the boss?

_____

_____

5. How much do you earn in an hour?

_____

_____

6. What do you do for fun?

_____

_____

7. What are your hobbies?

_____

_____

8. How do you spend your leisure time?

_____

_____

9. What does your home look like?

_____

_____

Spell out your preferences in detail. Write them down. Then put a copy of this worksheet someplace where you can see it periodically. Be prepared to discuss your description in class.

Assignment 11.3: Change Your Mind and Change Your Life

This chapter explained how changing your life from a "have to" to a "want to" basis allows you to get the changes you seek in your life. Usually time management is on a "have to" basis. Most likely you have not changed your procrastination habits regardless of the electronic time management devices you have purchased.

In this assignment, you will apply what you learned in this chapter on time and energy management skills.

1. Look again at the 24-hour chart you created in Assignment 11.1 to give yourself a realistic picture of your current use of your time and energy. Identify your current time and energy wasters and write them below:

    _____

    _____

    _____

    _____

    _____

    _____

    _____

    _____

    _____

    _____

    _____

(continued)

(continued)

2. Using any search engine, such as Google, find three articles on the Web that present you with the tools for change that you want to use to deal with your time and energy wasters. List these articles and their URLs below:

_____

_____

_____

_____

_____

_____

_____

_____

3. Write out your new tools in the form of three new time management goals or energy management goals:

1. _____

_____

_____

2. _____

_____

_____

3. _____

_____

_____

Save all this information to share with your class.

CHAPTER 12

Stress Management

"Success is directly proportional to how much stress you can gracefully endure. When you can deal with stress with joyous productivity, your blessings increase."

Karine Blackett

Stress can be defined as the way we react, positively or negatively, to physical and emotional change. In the 21st century, we are living our lives under a great deal of stress. People complain every day that they do not have enough time to accomplish all that they want to do. Most live very busy lives and can easily get caught up in those "stressful moments." Daily we receive a significant amount of negative news, and our lives just are not as simple as they used to be.

You as a student not only have stress from society, jobs, family, and friends, but also from academic challenges. This chapter looks at the physical and mental signs of stress and causes of stress and gives some great stress-reducing tips.

Types of Stress

Stress can be either positive or negative. Yes, there is such a thing as positive stress. The following sections discuss the differences between positive and negative stress.

Positive Stress

Positive stress, sometimes called *eustress,* is like an adrenalin rush. It can be energizing, motivating, and even lifesaving. The human stress response fuels us for athletic events, pressures us to earn money, and even yanks us out of harm's way when we find ourselves in danger. A certain amount of stress also can activate the creative subconscious to give ideas on how to successfully complete tasks or solve problems. It can help in attaining difficult goals and can even enhance performance. Total absence of stress would make life boring.

Negative Stress

Negative stress, sometimes referred to as *distress,* happens when stress exceeds a certain limit. It detracts from performance. It also can take its toll on both physical and mental health, causing many ailments.

Physical ailments caused by negative stress can include

- ❑ Frequent headaches
- ❑ Ulcers
- ❑ Hypertension
- ❑ Backache
- ❑ Shoulder and muscle tension
- ❑ Allergies
- ❑ Asthma
- ❑ Fatigue
- ❑ Insomnia
- ❑ Liver disease
- ❑ Heart disease
- ❑ Stroke
- ❑ Lowered immunity
- ❑ Obesity
- ❑ Change in vision
- ❑ Unexplained pain
- ❑ Nail biting, nervous tics, flinching

Mental ailments caused by negative stress include

❏ Anxiety

❏ Inability to concentrate

❏ Lack of appetite

❏ Depression

❏ Fear

❏ General irritability

❏ Forgetfulness

❏ Insomnia

❏ Tearfulness

❏ Confusion

Causes of Stress

There are many causes of stress. One of the biggest causes of stress is probably worry. Benjamin Franklin said, "Do not anticipate trouble or worry about what may never happen. Keep in the sunlight." As a student, you may have many worries. You might ask yourself hundreds of questions daily that can cause stress: Will I do well on my exam? Can I write a good paper? Can I go to school and still take care of my family? If you are an employee as well as a student, you might be worrying about the economy and your job. If you have a family to take care of, you might worry whether you are spending enough time with them while you are a student. You might be worried about a scholarship you need that will enable you to finish school. The list of the questions and concerns you have in your daily life could go on forever.

We like to think of worry as "what-ifs." We can "what if" ourselves to death. You know the common what-ifs you worry about: What if I don't pass the test? What if I don't get that scholarship? What if I can't get the student loan? What if my family doesn't think I am spending enough time with them since I am now in school and working? What if my job, school, and life just become too difficult? What if, what if, what if?

Do you know that over 90 percent of those things we worry about never happen? Don't you feel better already? We can hear those sighs of relief from way over here. Yet the fact remains that you can have stress in every part of your life. The following sections take a look at some of the major causes of stress, especially those causes that directly affect you as a student. These are found in your personal life, in the workplace, and in academics.

Stress in Your Personal Life

Your personal life can be the source of your greatest joys; it also can cause great stress. Do you have any of the following stressful events in your life right now?

❏ Marriage/separation/divorce

❏ Pregnancy/birth/death

❏ Personal injury or illness

❏ Loss of job/retirement

❏ Moving between homes/buying a house

❏ Changing jobs

❏ Change in financial status

❏ Relationship problems

❏ Deployment of loved ones

❏ Change in eating/sleeping habits

Stress in the Workplace

Another source of great fulfillment is work. However, it too can be very stressful. Do you experience stress from any of the following sources?

❏ Promotion

❏ Threat of redundancy (dismissal from a job, especially by layoff)

❏ Change in working hours or conditions

❏ Low pay

❏ Feeling of lack of control

❏ Lack of job satisfaction

❏ Personal friction/office politics

❑ Heavy workload or long working hours

❑ Sensory factors such as heat or noise

❑ Racism, sexism, or ageism

❑ Meeting deadlines

Stress from Academic Pursuits

You enrolled in school to improve your future, but attending school can make heavy demands on your time, energy, and mind. Do you experience any of these academic-related stresses?

❑ Overcoming a poor academic record

❑ Maintaining a certain GPA

❑ Being out of your comfort zone

❑ Competition with other students

❑ Increased difficulty in subject matter

❑ Increased pressure from difficult assignments

❑ Looking for additional sources of money to finance tuition

Ways to Relieve Stress

Stress relief is important. You cannot eliminate all the stress in your life, but you can reduce some of it.

Chapter 2, "Test-Taking Skills," gives tips for releasing stress when you are taking exams, and Chapter 5, "Attitude," gives advice on maintaining a positive attitude. Following those helpful tips will reduce some of your stress, but you should work on reducing stress in your life on a regular basis. The following sections give just a few quick pointers on how to reduce everyday stress, what we call the "stress busters."

Know Your Limits

Everyone's tolerance for stress is different, and every person handles stress in a different way. You will find it helpful to be aware of your stress limits.

Assignment 12.1: Determine Your Stress Level

Go to the Wellness.MA website and take a stress test. Find out how stressed out you really are:

www.wellness.ma/stress/stress-quiz.htm

Maintain Healthy Eating Habits

Nearly everyone is worried about weight, trying to find the quickest way of losing it. So many diets are out there today that deciding which one to follow is enough to cause stress. Doctors continue to recommend that we should quit all the fad diets and maintain healthful eating habits. This is good advice. Breakfast is still the most important meal of the day. You need fuel to think, and healthy food is fuel. Eating healthfully is a good habit. When you are eating healthfully, you may take longer to lose those unwanted pounds, but you are healthier while you're doing it.

If you have forgotten the infamous food pyramid and the types of food you should be eating, go to the following website sponsored by the U.S. Department of Health and Human Services, which gives some tips on maintaining a balanced, healthy diet:

www.health.gov/dietaryguidelines

However, the pyramid also promotes eating a great deal of bread and grains. You, like others, may find that a higher protein, lower carbohydrate diet fuels your brain and body better.

Exercise

Experts agree that exercising is one of the best ways to relieve stress. Exercising produces endorphins, which can reduce pain naturally and give you a feeling of relaxation and well-being. Exercise also can reduce blood pressure and help you fall asleep faster. Not only does it have these great positive effects on your body; it also can give you a few minutes of time alone with no phone, no doorbell, no kids, no bosses, and no instructors.

Taking the time to exercise is worth it. Join an aerobics class, an intra-mural sports program, or a cycling or weight training class, all of which involve about an hour, twice a week. Even a fifteen-minute brisk walk can help you reduce stress and keep in shape.

With your busy schedule, exercising may be difficult, but try to get into a regular exercise routine. Motivate yourself to exercise. Write affirmations about exercise, but don't forget to specify when and what. Don't just write, "I exercise." You need to write, "I eagerly exercise on Monday and Wednesday, taking a brisk walk at 1:00 p.m." When you write the affirmation positively, you tend to adhere to it. Remember that you *want* to exercise. Don't make it a "have to."

To learn more about stress relief and exercise, go to Paige Waehner's articles in the Exercise section of the About.com website:

> http://exercise.about.com/od/healthinjuries/a/stressrelief.htm

Stay Positive

We can't stress (oh, there's that word again) enough that having a posi-tive attitude definitely can help you reduce or even bypass stress. You *can* pass that exam. You *can* eat healthier. You *can* enjoy exercise.

Take Some Time for Yourself

Try to spend at least 10 to 15 minutes a day just on you. You can enjoy a cup of tea, light some candles, and just relax. A good time to do this is right after work or right after school.

Take a little time from your day to let go of the day's stressful events before interacting with your family or friends. Then you can face those you care about with a good positive attitude. They will appreciate it.

Don't use the excuse that you don't have time. Go back and read Chapter 11 on time management again. If you absolutely can't make it a daily routine, find 10 to 15 minutes every other day to spend on you.

Make Time for a Hobby

Gardening, painting, crafting, or tinkering in your garage can be great for stress relief. Many people will say they don't have time for a hobby. Planting flowers or a garden can take a little time in the beginning, but maintenance of that garden or flower bed takes only a few minutes each day or even a few minutes twice a week and gives you that time you need to just relax. You can take a few minutes to work on a quilt or crafting project each day. There is nothing that says you have to finish a craft as soon as you start it.

Listen to Relaxing Music

The emphasis in this stress buster is the phrase *relaxing music,* not the hardest rock band in the world. You may think that type of music releases stress and relaxes you, but it really doesn't. Hard rock may be your favorite music, but save it for the Friday night headbanger's ball or to energize you for studying if that works for you.

While you are cooking dinner, fixing something around the house, or driving in your car, listen to peaceful, easy listening music. Instead of listening to the nightly news, try putting on some nice, quiet music. The news is only going to cause you more stress, especially these days. Nothing is going to happen that you won't be able to read about online or in the newspaper tomorrow morning. If the world comes to an end, you will find out about it. Pass on the news and opt for some quiet or inspiring music.

For more information on the benefits of relaxing music, read Elizabeth Scott's article, "Music Relaxation: A Healthy and Convenient Stress Management Tool" at About.com:

http://stress.about.com/od/tensiontamers/a/musicrelaxation.htm

Holistic online.com also provides information about the stress-busting power of music:

http://holisticonline.com/stress/stress_music-therapy.htm

Meditate

Meditation is another great way to reduce stress. Many methods of meditation are available. Learning to use them takes practice, but meditation is worth learning. After you learn how to meditate, you can do it for short periods of time—even right before you take a test. Meditating will help you to relax, and the stress of the day will melt away. If you want to learn an easy method of meditation, do Assignment 12.2.

Assignment 12.2: Try Meditation

Complete the following steps:

1. Write a brief description of how you feel right now.

   _____

   _____

   _____

2. Go to the following website and read Gabriel Zappia's instructions on "How to Meditate":

   www.alternative-medicine.net/meditation/english.html

3. Practice the meditation a few times.

4. Write a brief description of how you feel after completing the exercise:

   _____

   _____

   _____

5. Compare your Before and After descriptions. Did the meditation have a positive effect on you? Write your response here:

   _____

   _____

   _____

Soak in the Tub

Soaking in warm water is a great stress reliever. Run a bathtub full of warm soapy water, add some relaxing bath infusions that contain lavender oil or chamomile, light some candles, turn on some quiet music, and get in the tub. Just relax. Shut your eyes and think about the music you are hearing. Practice the method of meditation you learned. Twenty minutes is all it takes.

Watch Bits and Pieces of a Favorite Movie

If you like movies and know which ones make you feel happy and uplifted, take a few minutes before you start to study or do an assignment to watch your favorite parts. You will feel good and be ready to conquer those assignments.

Treat Yourself to a Massage

Find a good masseuse in your town or city and treat yourself to a body massage about once every three months. It would be great to be able to do it more often, but massages can be a little pricey. Try to find someone who does pressure massage. It can be a little painful, but it puts you back into alignment as well as relaxing you. Pressure messages also can reduce headache pain and other annoying little aches and pains you may have. Many colleges and universities that offer massage therapy classes may have good deals on massages. Check out your local area schools and see whether they give discounts.

Use These Additional Stress Busters

Look for other small changes you can make to your life that will reduce stress. Following are some that we use.

- Breathe slowly.

- Avoid alcohol and drugs.

- Be prepared.

- Develop your study skills.

- Copy important papers you need.

- Use time management strategies.

- Keep a calendar.

- Network to get help when you need it.

- Set goals.

- Stop saying "Someday" and "Maybe things will be better tomorrow."

- Avoid negative people.

- Stop negative talk.

- Believe in yourself.
- Visualize success.
- Develop a sense of humor.
- Smile.
- Don't think you need to do it all or know it all.
- Say "No" more often.
- Look at problems as a challenge.
- Take in the beauty of the day or night.

Conclusion

You can choose which stress management tools to use to reduce your stress. Being a student and busy with jobs and family does cause a great deal of stress. Remember to eat healthy, exercise, and use other stress busters to reduce stress and make you a more productive and positive person. If you want to learn more about stress management, go to the websites we have listed. There are many resources listed in the appendix as well. Your local or school library probably has audio recordings or videos on stress management in addition to many self-help books on stress management. You can check them out at no cost, and they can be very helpful in reducing stress. Managing your stress levels will make your life much easier and make you a healthier and happier person and a more successful student.

Stress management completes our analysis and compilation of the 12 secrets for student success. Now that you know the 12 best practices for being a successful student, you will undoubtedly be head-and-shoulders above those who didn't take the opportunity to read them. Like any great recipe for success, we recommend that you take the ingredients and modify them to suit your particular life. The 12 success secrets will provide you with the foundation, and all 12 of these practices are related to your total success. If you use them, you will have the tools to go beyond your expectations for learning. These tools should not only increase what you get out of your academic experience, but also improve your success in everyday life.

We welcome hearing about your best practices in your classroom experience. Send your suggestions to us; we would like to include as many as possible in our next edition.

Best Practices: Stress Management

Do

- Do know that stress can cause illness.

- Do recognize when you are stressed.

- Do maintain a healthy diet.

- Do exercise regularly.

- Do stay positive.

- Do synergize.

- Do choose some stress busters and use them to reduce everyday stress.

Don't

- Don't worry.

- Don't let life get you down. You have the tools for success. Use them.

- Don't go it alone.

- Don't ignore signs of depression or severe stress—seek help.

Assignment 12.3: Experiment with More Stress Busters

Complete the following tasks:

1. Go to the following website and read through the 50 stress-busting techniques Philip Chave presents:

   www.distanthealer.co.uk/50_stress_busting_ideas_1.htm

2. Choose the one that you feel most relevant to you and write it here:

_____

_____

3. For one week, write a daily affirmation that states that you are applying that technique to your life. Write the first one here:

_____

_____

4. On the last day of that week, write a description of how the affirmation has affected you:

_____

_____

Websites, References, and Readings

Here is a critical-thinking tip for you: If you try one of the following Web links and you get an error, or it tells you the page can't be displayed, don't despair. Sometimes links reference a page that extends past the .com, .net, or .org address. Those file locations to the right of the .com, .net, .org can sometimes change. If you can't get to the page you want, try erasing any part of the address that appears after the .com, .net, .org, and so on. Suppose you want to get to the following website:

www.howtostudy.com/studtips.htm

This page is supposed to give some great study tips, but all you seem to get is an error message. Delete the /studtips.htm and just use this:

www.howtostudy.com

That address should get you to the page you need. Then you can do a search on the Web page for "study tips." (We learned this trick when we were trying to keep links updated on our websites.)

Following is another idea that may help you: If you want to search for more information on any of the success tips we have given you, use Yahoo!,

Note: The sites listed in this appendix can be helpful to you as far as studying, stress management, test taking, attitude, and so on. Just remember: Don't use them for doing a research paper. What resources should you use for your paper? Use the electronic resources provided to you by the school you attend.

Google, or another good Internet search engine. Type what you are looking for in the Search text box. You should get a list of sites that can be helpful.

We hope the following information will continue to help you in your goal of enhancing your academic success.

Chapter 1: Study Skills

Websites

http://712educators.about.com/od/creativethinking/tp/mnemonics.htm—Mnemonic devices

http://artchavez.net/survey—Study skills assessment

http://theelearningcoach.com/elearning_design/chunking-information—Chunking tips

www.allsands.com/Science/mnemonicdevices_soa_gn.htm—Mnemonic devices

www.csbsju.edu/Academic-Advising/Study-Skills-Guide.htm—Study skills guide

www.english-zone.com/study/symbols.html—Note-taking symbols

www.essortment.com/family/survivingfirst_seps.htm—Surviving the first year of college

www.howtostudy.com/topten.htm —Top ten study tips

www.howtostudy.org—Study guides and writing help

www.lhps.org/studyskills/page3.htm—Note-taking skills

www.mindtools.com/pages/article/newISS_01.htm—Mind maps

www.mindtools.com/pages/main/newMN_ISS.htm—Learning skills

www.mtsu.edu/~studskl/10tips.html—College survival tips

www.mtsu.edu/~studskl/mem.html—Memory skills

www.richland.edu/james/misc/testtake.html—Math study help

www.studygs.net/tsttak1.htm—Study guides

www.studyguidezone.com/—Study tips

www.study-skills-for-all-ages.com/mind-mapping.html—Mind mapping

www.ucc.vt.edu/stdysk/checklis.html—Study skills checklist

www.usu.edu/arc/idea_sheets/pdf/mnemonic_dev.pdf—
Mnemonic devices

Additional Resources

Fry, R. (2004). *How to study* (6th edition). Delmar Cengage Learning.

Fry, R. (1999). *The great big book of how to study*. Delmar Cengage Learning.

Kesselman-Turkel, J. & Peterson, F. (2003). *Note-taking made easy*. University of Wisconsin Press.

Paul, K. (2009). *Study smarter, not harder* (3rd edition). Vancouver, BC: Self-Counsel Press.

Roberts, L. & Pritchard, L. (2004). Skills give students a spring in their step. *Times Higher Education Supplement*, 0(1622): 25.

Robinson, A. (1993). *What smart students know: Maximum grades. Optimum learning. Minimum time*. New York: Three Rivers Press.

Siebert, A. & Karr, M. (2008). *The adult student's guide to survival & success* (6th edition). Practical Psychology Press.

Siegle, D. (2004, Spring). The merging of literacy and technology in the 21st century. *Gifted Child Today*, 27(2): 32.

Weathers, B. (2004, February). Learning to learn: Student activities for developing work, study and exam-writing skills. *Teacher Librarian*, 32(3): 35.

Yates, J. & Yates, C. (2004). Freshman study guide. *Campus Life*, 62(7): 50–53.

Videos: YouTube has many videos that are geared toward college success. If you go to www.youtube.com and type in "study strategies for college," you will get a list of many videos that can help you with your study skills. These videos will help you understand the concepts in Chapter 1.

Chapter 2: Test-Taking Skills

Websites

http://frank.mtsu.edu/~studskl/teststrat.html—Survival strategies for taking tests

http://test-anxiety.com—Addressing test anxiety

www.bucks.edu/~specpop/tests.htm—Test-taking strategies

www.d.umn.edu/student/loon/acad/strat/test_take.html—Test-taking tips

www.englishcompanion.com/room82/testingskills.html—Test-taking skills

www.how-to-study.com/study-skills/en/taking-tests/47/test-anxiety—Test anxiety

www.learningskills.com/test.html—Test anxiety measurement

www.prenhall.com/success/StudySkl/testtake.html—Test-taking tips

www.studygs.net/tstprp6.htm—Organizing for test taking

www.testtakingtips.com—Test-taking tips

www.ulc.psu.edu/studyskills/test_taking.html—Test preparation, test anxiety, and test-taking tips

www.wwu.edu/depts/chw/student_health/publications/test_strategies_info.pdf—Test strategies

www.wright.edu/cps/studentsuccess/testanxiety.htm—Test anxiety workshop

Additional Resources

Kesselman-Turkel, J. & Peterson, F. (2004). *Test taking strategies* (2nd edition). University of Wisconsin Press.

Newman, E. (1996). *No more test anxiety: Effective steps for taking tests and achieving better grades.* Los Angeles, CA: Learning Skills Publications.

Nugent, P. & Vitale, B. (2008). *Test success: Test taking techniques for beginning nursing students* (5th edition). F. A. Davis Company.

Rozakis, L. (2002). *Test-taking strategies & study skills for the utterly confused.* New York: McGraw-Hill.

Videos: YouTube offers many videos on test-taking skills and test anxiety. Go to www.youtube.com and type in "test-taking strategies" or "test anxiety." You will see several videos that are available to help you be a more successful test taker. These videos will help you understand the concepts in Chapter 2.

Chapter 3: Perception, Learning Styles, and Personality

Websites

http://typelogic.com—Personality assessment information

www.colorquiz.com—Color and personality

www.humanmetrics.com—Personality assessment information

www.ldpride.net/learning-style-test-b.html—Learning styles assessment

www.mindtools.com/mnemlsty.html—Learning style information

www.personalitybook.com/page/registration/userreg.xml—Personality assessment

www.usd.edu/trio/tut/ts/style.html—Learning style information

Additional Resources

Baron, R. (1998). *What type am I? Discover who you really are.* New York: Penguin Books.

Berens, L. & Nardi, D. (1999). *The 16 personality types: Descriptions for self-discovery.* Huntington Beach, CA: Telos Publications.

Dembo, M. & Seli, H. (2007). *Motivation and learning strategies for college success: A self-management approach* (3rd edition). Routledge.

McCoy, D. (2008). *Your ultimate personality quiz: 500 fun & fascinating questions—All about you!* Sourcebooks.

Tieger, P. & Barron-Tieger, B. (2007). *Do what you are: Discover the perfect career for you through the secrets of personality type* (4th revised and updated edition). Little, Brown and Company.

Weiner, I. & Greene, R. (2007). *Handbook of personality assessment.* Wiley.

Videos: If you go to YouTube, there are several videos available about learning styles and personality. Just type in "learning styles" or "personality types," and you will see several links to short videos about these subjects. These videos will help you understand the concepts in Chapter 3.

Chapter 4: Organization

Websites

http://aresty.rutgers.edu/gettingorganized.htm—Online resources for getting organized

http://lifeorganizers.com/cm_articles/45_help_students_get_ organized_335.html—A helpful site for getting organized at school

http://wethersfield.k12.ct.us/High_School/fresh_study_book.pdf— Study and organizational skills

www.associatedcontent.com/article/810759/how_to_stay_organized_ in_college.html?cat=4—Staying organized in college

www.ehow.com/how_2300233_stay-organized-college.html—Staying organized in college

www.findingdulcinea.com/guides/Education/College-Living.pg_ 00.html—Getting organized for college life

www.iol.ie/~stjsrbge/studyskills.htm—Organization and study skills

www.jimwrightonline.com/php/interventionista/interventionista_intv_ list.php?prob_type=study___skills__organization—Organization and study skills

www.mindtools.com/pages/article/newHTE_05.htm—Using to-do lists

www.mindtools.com/pages/article/newLDR_98.htm—Delegating

www.mindtools.com/pages/article/newPPM_01.htm—Making time estimates

www.muskingum.edu/~cal/database/general/organization.html— Organization skills for studying

www.nlight.com/Success/Study/3organize.html—Getting organized in college

www.studygs.net/orgstr1.htm—Organizing projects

Additional Resources

Fry, R. (2004). *Get organized* (3rd edition). Delmar Cengage Learning.

Worthington, J. & Farrar, R. (1998). *The ultimate college survival guide* (4th edition). Princeton, NJ: Peterson's.

Videos: YouTube has several videos available about organization and study tips. Just type in "study organization tips," and you will see several links to short videos about these subjects. If you are a visual learner, these videos will help you understand the concepts in Chapter 4.

Chapter 5: Attitude

Websites

http://emotiontoolkit.com/journal/index.php?s=positive+thinking—Changing your thinking

http://ezinearticles.com/?Success-Intelligence-:-Attitudes-to-Success&id=64069—Attitude of success

http://positiveteens0.tripod.com/positivethinking—Positive living tips

www.exforsys.com/career-center/attitude-development/a-good-attitude-leads-to-success.html—Attitude development

www.marin.edu/~don/Study/2positive.html—Positive self-talk

www.mayoclinic.com/health/positive-thinking/SR00009—Health benefits of positive thinking

www.personal-development.com/chuck/attitude.htm—Definition of attitude

www.successconsciousness.com/index_000009.htm—Positive thinking

www.successconsciousness.com/positive_attitude.htm—Positive attitude

Additional Resources

Fritz, R. (2008). *The power of a positive attitude: Discovering the key to success.* AMACOM.

Hay, L. (2004). *Everyday positive thinking.* Hay House Publishers.

Hill, N. & Stone, W. (2007). *Success through a positive mental attitude.* Pocket Publishing.

Maxwell, J. (2006). *The difference maker: Making your attitude your greatest asset.* Nashville, TN: Thomas Nelson, Inc.

Maxwell, J. (2003). *Attitude 101: What every leader needs to know.* Nashville, TN: Thomas Nelson, Inc.

Morris, G. (2010). *7 days to a positive attitude: A one-week game plan for beginning the journey toward brighter days* (updated edition). Blue Mountain Arts.

Orloff, J. (2009). *Emotional freedom: Liberate yourself from negative emotions and transform your life.* Three Rivers Press.

Peale, N. (2005). *The power of positive thinking and the amazing results of positive thinking collection.* Simon & Schuster.

Videos: YouTube offers several videos about attitude. Type in "positive attitude" and/or "positive thinking" in the Search bar to see several links to short videos about the subjects talked about in Chapter 5.

Chapter 6: Goal Setting

Websites

http://academic.cuesta.edu/acasupp/as/202.HTM—Goal setting advice

http://lac.smccme.edu/goalsetting.htm—Goal setting and motivation

http://studyskills.suite101.com/article.cfm/smart_goals_for_college_students—SMART goals for college students

www.brighthub.com/education/online-learning/articles/46272.aspx—Goal setting for online learners

www.brookhavencollege.edu/studentsvcs/counseling/goal-setting.aspx—Basic goal setting information

www.ehow.com/video_4756571_setting-academic-goals.html—Setting academic goals video

www.exsel.mtu.edu/UN1000/Activities/Goal%20Setting%20Activity.pdf—Goal setting activities

www.goal-setting-guide.com/smart-goals.html—SMART goals

www.mindtools.com/pages/article/newHTE_06.htm—Goal setting tools

www.mygoals.com—Goal setting ideas

www.mygoals.com/content/college-goals.html—Setting goals for college

Additional Resources

Dobson, M. & Wilson, S. (2008). *Goal setting: How to create an action plan and achieve your goals* (2nd edition). AMACOM.

Koestner, R., Lekes, N. & Powers, T. (2002, July). Attaining personal goals: Self-concordance plus implementation intentions equals success. *Journal of Personality and Social Psychology,* 83(1): 231.

Tracy, B. (2010). *Goals!: How to get everything you want—Faster than you ever thought possible* (2nd edition). Berrett-Koehler Publishers.

Videos: YouTube (www.youtube.com) has several videos available on goal setting. Just type in "goal setting" in the Search bar, and you will see several links to short videos about this subject. These videos will help you understand the concepts in Chapter 6.

Chapter 7: Basic Research Skills

Websites

http://library.byuh.edu/research—Research help

www.bbk.ac.uk/lib/about/learn/research—Library research skills online tutorial

www.ithacalibrary.com/research—Research tips

www.ipl.org—Online library

www.lib.washington.edu/uwill/research101/basic00.htm—Basic research skills

www.library.cornell.edu/olinuris/ref/tutorialsguides.html—Guide to library research

www.muskingum.edu/~cal/database/general/writing.html—Writing skills www.shambles.net/pages/learning/infolit/research—Library research

www.thinkquest.org/library—Websites created by students for students

Additional Resources

Ercegovac, Z. (2008). *Information literacy: Search strategies, tools and resources for high school students and college freshmen.* Linworth Publishing.

George, M. (2008). *The elements of library research: What every student needs to know.* Princeton University Press.

Quaratiello, A. & Devine, J. (2010). *College student's research companion: Finding, evaluating, and citing the resources you need to succeed* (fifth edition). Neal-Schuman Publishers.

Riedling, A. (2006). *Learning to learn: A guide to becoming information literate in the 21st century* (2nd edition). Neal-Schuman Publishers.

Schunk, D. & Zimmerman, B. (1998). *Self-regulated learning: From teaching to self-reflective practice.* New York: Guilford Press.

Videos: Several videos about library research skills are available on YouTube. Type in one of the following terms at www.youtube.com for a list of videos under those headings: library research skills, electronic resources, research skills, or library research for college students. You will see several links to short videos about the subjects talked about in Chapter 7.

Chapter 8: Research Paper Writing

Websites

http://owl.english.purdue.edu—Great resource for research paper help

www.ehow.com/how_9263_write-research-paper.html—Tips on how to write a research paper

www.gc.maricopa.edu/English/topicarg.html—Topics for research papers

www.ruf.rice.edu/~bioslabs/tools/report/reportform.html—Help on writing papers

www.ucc.vt.edu/stdysk/termpapr.html—Process for writing a paper

www.wisc.edu/writing/Handbook/PlanResearchPaper.html—Planning and writing a research paper

Additional Resources

Ellison, C. (2010). *McGraw-Hill's concise guide to writing research papers*. McGraw-Hill.

Lester, J. & Lester Jr., J. (2009). *Writing research papers* (13th edition). Longman Publishing.

Rozakis, L. (2007). *Schaum's quick guide to writing research papers* (2nd edition). McGraw-Hill.

Strunk Jr., W. (2009). *Elements of style*. Walking Lion Press.

Winkler, A. and McCuen-Metherell, J. (2009). *Writing the research paper: A handbook* (7th edition). Wadsworth Publishing.

Videos: YouTube offers several videos about writing research papers. Type in "writing research papers" at www.youtube.com for a list of videos dealing with that subject. You will see several links to short videos about the subjects in Chapter 8. We especially recommend the following two videos about citing in APA style:

www.youtube.com/watch?v=9pbUoNa5tyY

www.youtube.com/watch?v=7HsYUA-helk

Chapter 9: Synergy

Websites

http://en.wikipedia.org/wiki/Synergy—Definition of synergy

www.adventureassoc.com/resources/team-work-skills/teamwork-skills.html—Activities for team building

www.buzzle.com/articles/team-building-activities-for-students.html—Team building exercises

www.collegetips.com—Survival tips for college students

www.ehow.com/how_5670728_good-college-academic-advisor.html—Academic advisors

www.gocollege.com/survival—College survival tips

www.how-to-study.com/study-skills/en/studying/38/study-groups—Tips on study groups www.mycollegetips.com/tips-roommate.html—Getting along with roommates

www.mycollegetips.com/tips-social-life.html—Tips for getting to know other students

Additional Resources

Bernstein, M. (2010). *How to survive your freshman year* (4th edition). Hundreds of Heads Books.

Cohen, H. (2011). *The naked roommate: And 107 other issues you might run into in college* (4th edition). Sourcebooks.

Fitzgerald, S. & Peters, J. (2011). *The everything college survival book: All you need to get the most out of college life* (3rd edition). Adams Media.

Videos: If you go to YouTube, you can find several videos about synergy. Type in one of the following terms at www.youtube.com for a list of videos under those headings: academic advising, how to get along with a roommate in college, tutoring for college students, or college survival. You will see several links to short videos about the subjects in Chapter 9.

Chapter 10: Motivation

Websites

http://gwired.gwu.edu/counsel/index.gw/Site_ID/5176/Page_ID/14139/—Motivation tips

www.assessmentgenerator.com/H/cRboslearn1171904074.html—Student motivation survey

www.ccri.edu/advising/success_links/motivation.html—Top ten motivation tips

www.eslteachersboard.com/cgi-bin/motivation/index.pl—Links to articles on motivation

www.philforhumanity.com/Five_Motivational_Tips.html—Motivational tips

www.ucc.vt.edu/stdysk/motivate.html—Motivational tools

Additional Resources

Chandler, S. (2004). *100 ways to motivate yourself: Change your life forever.* Franklin Lakes, NJ: Career Press.

Fiore, N. (2010). *Awaken your strongest self* (2nd edition). McGraw-Hill.

Harrell, K. (2005). *Attitude is everything: 10 life-changing steps to turning attitude into action.* New York: Harper Business.

Johnson, J. (2006). *The sixty-second motivator.* Dog Ear Publishing.

Luciani, J. (2004). *The power of self-coaching: The five essential steps to creating the life you want.* Wiley.

Videos: YouTube has several videos about self-motivation. Type in "self motivation" or "motivation for college students" in the Search bar at www.youtube.com for a list of links to short videos about the subjects in Chapter 10.

Chapter 11: Time and Energy Management

Websites

http://gradschool.about.com/cs/timemanagement/a/time.htm—Mastering your time

http://studyskills.suite101.com/article.cfm/time_management_for_students—Time management

www.cob.sjsu.edu/nellen_a/time_management.htm—Time management tips

www.d.umn.edu/kmc/student/loon/acad/strat/time_man_princ.html—Time management principles

www.dartmouth.edu/~acskills/success/time.html—Managing time

www.mindtools.com/pages/main/newMN_HTE.htm—Tools for time management

www.studygs.net/timman.htm—Time management strategies

www.time-management-for-students.com/Tracking_Your_Time.php—Time tracking advice

www.time-management-guide.com/prioritizing.html—Prioritizing

www.time-management-guide.com/student-time-management.html—
Time management guide

www.ucc.vt.edu/lynch/TMActivity.htm—Time management activity

Additional Resources

Berk, R. (2009). *The five-minute time manager for college students.* Coventry Press.

Brown, D. B. (2010). *Time management for college students: How to manage school, work, and fun!* Learning Life eBooks.

Leland, K. & Bailey, K. (2008). *Time management in an instant: 60 ways to make the most of your day.* Career Press.

Mackenzie, A. & Nickerson, P. (2009). *The time trap: The classic book on time management* (4th edition). AMACOM.

Scharf, D., Schard, D., & Hait, P. (2004). *Studying smart: Time management for college students.* Barnes & Noble.

Tracy, B. (2007). *Eat that frog: 21 great ways to stop procrastinating and get more done in less time* (2nd edition). San Francisco, CA: Berrett-Koehler Publishers, Inc.

Zeller, D. (2009). *Successful time management for dummies.* Wiley.

Videos: YouTube has several videos available on time management. Type in one of the following subjects at www.youtube.com for a list of videos: time management, time management for college students, or managing your time. You will see several links to short videos about the subjects talked about in Chapter 11.

Chapter 12: Stress Management

Websites

http://stress.about.com—Stress-related information and blog

http://stress.about.com/od/programsandpractices/a/exercise.htm—
Stress relief through exercises

www.aetna.com/health-wellness—Wellness information

www.conqueringstress.com/stress_management_techniques.html—Conquering stress

www.conqueringstress.com/stress-remedies.html—Stress remedies

www.essortment.com/lifestyle/herbalbathbene_snxo.htm—Herbal bath recipes

www.fi.edu/learn/heart/healthy/diet.html—Healthy heart diet

www.healthvideo.com—Health and wellness videos and articles

www.healthyeating.net—Information on nutrition, food guides, and health

www.helpguide.org/life/healthy_eating_diet.htm—Healthy diet information

www.helpguide.org/mental/stress_management_relief_coping.htm—Coping with stress

www.mayoclinic.com/health/exercise-and-stress/SR00036—Exercising to combat stress

www.mftrou.com/stress-management-techniques.html—Seven top stress management techniques

www.mindtools.com/smpage.html—Stress management techniques

www.mindtools.com/pages/main/newMN_TCS.htm—Stress management tools

www.optimalhealthconcepts.com/Stress—Emotional wellness links

www.prevention.com/health—Healthy living

www.stress-relief-exercises.com—Exercises for stress relief

www.tuesdaytoasters.org/tips/relax.html—Relaxation tips

www.webmd.com/diet—Healthy eating and diet

www.wellness.com—Information on wellness

Additional Resources

Bowden, J. (2008). *The 150 most effective ways to boost your energy: The surprising unbiased truth about using nutrition, exercise, supplements, stress relief, and personal empowerment to stay energized all day.* Fair Winds Press.

Bowden, J. (2007). *The 150 healthiest foods on earth: The surprising, unbiased truth about what you should eat and why.* Fair Winds Press.

Davis, M., Robbins, E., & McKay, M. (2008). *The relaxation & stress reduction workbook* (6th edition). New Harbinger Publications.

Epstein, R. (2000). *The big book of stress relief games.* McGraw-Hill.

Nurriestearns, M. (2010). *Yoga for anxiety: Meditations and practices for calming the body.* New Harbinger Press.

Posen, Dr. D. (2009). *The little book of stress relief.* Key Porter Books.

Stahl, B. & Goldstein, E. (2010). *A mindfulness-based stress reduction work book.* New Harbinger Publications.

Truman, K. (1991). *Feelings buried alive never die* (4th edition). Salt Lake City, UT: Brigham Distributing.

Wehrenberg, M. (2008). *The 10 best-ever anxiety management techniques: Understanding how your brain makes you anxious and what you can do to change it.* W.W. Norton and Company.

Wheeler, C. (2007). *10 simple solutions to stress: How to tame tension and start enjoying your life.* New Harbinger Publications.

Videos: Several videos on stress management are available on YouTube. Type in one of the following subjects at www.youtube.com for a list of videos: stress management techniques, stress management, healthy eating, stress reducing exercises, or stress relief yoga. You will see several links to short videos about the subjects talked about in Chapter 12.

Index